CAPSTONE

G000123345

Stay Sn...

Smart Things to Know About **Brands and Branding**	JOHN MARIOTTI
Smart Things to Know About **Business**	JAMES LEIBERT
Smart Things to Know About **Business Finance**	KEN LANGDON
Smart Things to Know About **Change**	DAVID FIRTH
Smart Things to Know About **Consultancy**	PATRICK FORSYTH
Smart Things to Know About **CRM**	DAVID HARVEY
Smart Things to Know About **Culture**	DONNA DEEPROSE
Smart Things to Know About **Customers**	ROS JAY
Smart Things to Know About **Decision Making**	KEN LANGDON
Smart Things to Know About **E-Business**	MIKE CUNNINGHAM
Smart Things to Know About **E-commerce**	MIKE CUNNINGHAM
Smart Things to Know About **Growth**	TONY GRUNDY
Smart Things to Know About **Innovation and Creativity**	DENNIS SHERWOOD
Smart Things to Know About **Knowledge Management**	THOMAS KOULOPOULOS
Smart Things to Know About **Leadership**	JONATHAN YUDELOWITZ
Smart Things to Know About **Life Long-learning**	ANDREW HOLMES
Smart Things to Know About **Managing Projects**	DONNA DEEPROSE
Smart Things to Know About **Marketing**	JOHN MARIOTTI
Smart Things to Know About **Mergers & Acquisitions**	TONY GRUNDY
Smart Things to Know About **Motivation**	DONNA DEEPROSE
Smart Things to Know About **Partnerships**	JOHN MARIOTTI
Smart Things to Know About **People Management**	DAVID FIRTH
Smart Things to Know About **Scenario Planning**	TONY KIPPENBERGER
Smart Things to Know About **Six Sigma**	ANDREW BERGER
Smart Things to Know About **Strategy**	RICHARD KOCH
Smart Things to Know About **Managing Talent**	STEPHANIE OVERMAN
Smart Things to Know About **Teams**	ANNEMARIE CARRACIOLO
Smart Things to Know About **Technology Management**	ANDREW HOLMES
Smart Things to Know About **Your Career**	JOHN MIDDLETON

CAPSTONE

Smart

THINGS TO KNOW ABOUT

Technology
Management

ANDREW HOLMES

First published 2003 by

Capstone Publishing Ltd (A John Wiley & Sons Co.)
8 Newtec Place
Magdalen Road
Oxford OX4 1RE
United Kingdom
http://www.capstoneideas.com

British Library Cataloguing in Publication Data
A CIP catalogue record for this book is available from the British Library

ISBN 1-84112-426-5

Typeset by
Forewords, 109 Oxford Road, Cowley, Oxford

Printed and bound by
T.J. International Ltd, Padstow, Cornwall

This book is printed on acid-free paper

Contents

What is Smart?

The *Smart* series is a new way of learning. *Smart* books will improve your understanding and performance in some of the critical areas you face to-day like *customers, strategy, change, e-commerce, brands, influencing skills, knowledge management, finance, teamworking, partnerships.*

Smart books summarize accumulated wisdom as well as providing original cutting-edge ideas and tools that will take you out of theory and into action.

The widely respected business guru Chris Argyris points out that even the most intelligent individuals can become ineffective in organizations. Why? Because we are so busy working that we fail to learn about ourselves. We stop reflecting on the changes around us. We get sucked into the patterns of behavior that have produced success for us in the past, not realizing that it may no longer be appropriate for us in the fast-approaching future.

There are three ways the Smart series helps prevent this happening to you:

- by increasing your self-awareness

- by developing your understanding, attitude and behavior

- by giving you the tools to challenge the status quo that exists in your organization.

Smart people need smart organizations. You could spend a third of your career hopping around in search of the Holy Grail, or you could begin to create your own smart organization around you today.

Finally a reminder that books don't change the world, people do. And although the *Smart* series offers you the brightest wisdom from the best practitioners and thinkers, these books throw the responsibility on you to *apply* what you're learning in your work.

Because the truly smart person knows that reading a book is the start of the process and not the end . . .

As Eric Hoffer says, "In times of change, learners inherit the world, while the learned remain beautifully equipped to deal with a world that no longer exists."

David Firth
Smartmaster

Introduction

Technology: It's Time For Us To Manage It, Not It To Manage Us

Before I start, it is important to make the point that throughout this book I will talk about technology management and IT in the same vein, as I will within this introduction. This is because for organizations, technology management increasingly means IT, and it is IT that is one of the most disruptive technologies to enter the organization. The concepts and ideas expressed in this book are therefore principally focused on IT.

SMART QUOTES

The thing with high-tech is that you always end up using scissors.

David Hockney

So you think we're in control?

Ever since the Stone Age, man has attempted to harness technology in whatever form it took to enhance their lives. From the invention of the wheel, to the creation of the computer we have used technology to eliminate the mundane, boring and manually intensive aspects of our lives. Up until recently we have been in control of the technology, determining how and when it would be applied. Nowadays, it seems that technology is in control of us. This is particularly the case when we look at the effect that technology has had on the world of work.

> The acceleration of change in our time is, itself, an elemental force. This accelerative thrust has personal psychological, as well as sociological consequences.
>
> Alvin Toffler

While in the home the application of technology in all its guises has been a godsend – labour-saving devices have made our daily lives less tiresome and manually intensive – within the world of work it has not been such a happy affair. Unbeknown to its inventors, the emergence of the computer and IT in the late 1940s was to have a profound effect on the world of work and one that continues to impact us all. The rapidity of change, driven in the main by technological change and connectivity, has meant that we are increasingly unable to manage it as well as we should. Some of this mismanagement is due to incompetence and poor management practices, but a lot is down to our inability to manage the consequences of rapid and continuous change. This makes the management of technology all the more important. However, unlike the past, where we were the masters of technology, it appears that we are now its

SMART VOICES

New technology tells bar staff to clean up

A recent article in *The Age*, an Australian daily newspaper, described a new technology called iGlass. iGlass is a wireless sensing system that measures the level of liquid in a glass and transmits this to bar staff. So, when a customer's glass is empty, a member of staff can go pick it up. The system can distinguish between liquid and ice, so even if your glass is only left with ice, it will still be retrieved. The glassware has a tiny microprocessor and electrode embedded in a screw-off base and thin copper electrodes running up the sides of the glass. The microprocessor will measure the amount of liquid left in the glass and transmit this to bar staff via the customer's table. The table contains an electrical coil that generates a small, oscillating magnetic field that powers the glasses and transmits the information. No more empty glasses cluttering up the table.

(L. Johnson, *The Age*, 24 Jun. 2002)

slaves. Just consider your own working life and how it is now, to a greater or lesser extent, defined by technology. As you walk through the door and fire up your PC, you are in the hands of technology. When it fails, you feel helpless. When it does not work you feel angry. And yet without it you are naked. That's the reality of our working lives, so we had better get used to it and we had better begin to manage and control it more effectively than we do now. Unfortunately, when it comes to technology management we have plenty of issues to deal with.

Welcome to the electronic sweatshop

Unfortunately, the academics of the 1950s were wide of the mark when they predicted that we would find ourselves in what they described as the leisure society, in which we would be unencumbered with work and basically doing whatever we wanted. Technology would have created a world in which we would want for nothing, everything would run smoothly because it was controlled by computer technology. Instead we are faced with longer working hours and job spill, where our working time literally spills over into our leisure time. So much for the leisure society. For example, Americans are working longer and harder than ever before – 25 million now work more than 49 hours a week, with a large number working a lot more; 11 million spend 60 hours or more at work. The same is true for the United Kingdom which has the longest working hours in Europe; 91 per cent of British managers now work more than their contracted hours. Another study of working couples showed that almost half of men and over a third of women were working more hours than they wanted to. The increasing hours spent at the office is mirrored by the amount of work that is conducted outside of traditional working hours, mainly at home or on the commute to and from work. Such job spill impacts our leisure time and invades family life. For example, 39 per cent of Americans no longer take lunch breaks, instead favouring to work through to keep up with their work.

In particular, commuting "dead time" is becoming an extension of the working day, made possible by cellular phones, laptops and wireless links to the office. As expected, longer working hours, both inside and outside of work, means that there is less time to unwind. With work

SMART QUOTES

Technology is changing the way we work, demanding more of us, requiring new skills and setting new problems. It has given us great freedom, access to enormous volumes of information, and has destroyed distance. . . . It has led to understanding but also increased confusion and alarm, not least about the effects of globalization that is changing the trading patterns, economics and employment opportunities of the world.

Gerry Barker

spilling over to weekends and evenings, white-collar workers are finding themselves squeezed, with little or no time to relax and recover from the working day. Despite the additional time spent working, Americans are finding it ever more difficult to keep up with demanding schedules. According to the American Management Association, almost 50 per cent of Americans now feel stressed at work. Stress is a way of life for many white-collar workers irrespective of age or position within the corporate hierarchy. This is in part driven by the feeling of fear of losing their jobs if they are not seen to be keeping up. What typically happens in America usually occurs elsewhere too, as the most technologically advanced nation it is the United States that is the vanguard of the technological change that ultimately affects us all. So, despite the introduction of computers in the workplace, which were designed to improve productivity and make the organization run like a well-oiled machine, they have created a major headache and overhead that was never envisaged. This is in part due to the massive amounts of information that now flows across the organization.

In the last twenty years the amount of time Americans have spent at their jobs has risen steadily. Each year the change is small amounting to about nine hours, or slightly more than one additional day of work. In any given year, such a small increment has probably been imperceptible. But the accumulated increase over two decades is substantial. When surveyed, Americans report that they have only sixteen and a half hours of leisure a week, after obligations of job and household are taken care of. Working hours are already longer than they were forty years ago. If present trends continue, by the end of the century Americans will be spending as much time at their jobs as they did back in the nineteen twenties.

Juliet Schor

Information explosion

Information is the life-blood of the modern corporation: in 1990 the typical Fortune 500 company stored 33 billion characters of electronic data, and in 2010 this is expected to be 400 trillion (Wind and Main, 1998). To achieve such a significant increase in data over such a comparatively short space of time, it will have to grow by a compound rate of 60 per cent per annum, which is phenomenal. According to the US analyst, the Meta Group, the volume of corporate information is doubling every twelve months, and is accelerating (Newing, 1999). The message that such projections portray is significant – as organizations produce more and more data, it can very rapidly spiral out of control, especially when there is no one to keep it in check, to ensure it is the right data, that it is current, accurate and adding value. Furthermore, as the lines of communication within organizations have become more sophisticated, the amount of information to process has increased, and, more importantly, so has the time required to make decisions. What is in no doubt is that information in the modern corporation is growing, and growing fast. Organizations have an insatiable appetite for it as they drive to seek customer satisfaction, increase market share and improve operational efficiencies. If being in business is all about gaining and retaining customers and providing them with the products and services they need, then information, and lots of it, is what organizations need. But, organizations should take great care. Although lots of information can add value, if it is wrong, or managed incompetently, then investments in the IT infrastructure required to support it may be wasted.

This massive increase in information leads to some real problems, including:

> **SMART QUOTES**
>
> We are not in the Information Age, but in an age of information.
>
> John McKean

- *Information overload.* Information overload is often fuelled by organizations that constantly update their IT infrastructures to accept more and more data. In addition, as electronic mail flies around the organization in ever-increasing volumes, the amount of information that people have to contend with is increasing sharply. People are literally drowning in data. The increasing bandwidth of networks is tempting users to gather far more information than they actually need. This exacerbates information overload, with people not knowing what information they need to make decisions. Less, not more information is required. But the message doesn't seem to be getting through.

- *Information politics.* Although fuelled by an increasing dependence on knowledge, the most important driver for the increase in information has been the changes within organizations that followed the downsizing of the early-to-mid-1990s. With the loss of positional and status power, employees have realized that information and knowledge is power and

---

Q. If data and information are so important, how can I manage them?

A. Introducing an information lifecycle can be very helpful because it forces the enterprise to view their information as an asset. It also helps them to retire legacy systems that retain information that is no longer required. The key is to tie information needs into business and strategic planning. The information lifecycle has six stages:

1. Business and strategic planning.
2. Assess information requirements.
3. Capture information.
4. Develop technology solutions to deliver the information.
5. Use and apply information.
6. Retire information and systems.

SMART
ANSWERS
TO TOUGH
QUESTIONS

they will guard it jealously. For example, a recent study found that 20 per cent of UK employees believe that it is not in their best interests to share knowledge, preferring to hoard it to win promotion, or move to another employer (Fran, 2000).

- *Poor data integrity.* With increasing volumes of information, the ability to control its integrity and accuracy is becoming harder. Most organizations are unaware of how accurate their data is or whether it is adding any value. Data that is of poor quality or out of date leads to poor decision making. And the failure to retire information that is no longer needed leads to additional IT costs associated with systems that should be decommissioned.

Increasing volumes of information would not have been possible without the acceleration of technology, and it is to this we now turn.

The acceleration of technology

There can be no doubt that computers were probably the most important technology to have emerged in the twentieth century. In the space of forty years, they became central to the efficient operation of most industrialized nations. Indeed, it is now recognized that many industries, organizations and government bodies could not operate efficiently, and in some cases at all, without them. A significant proportion of organizations can therefore be considered IT-centric. That is, their ability to function within the increasingly competitive global economy is only possible through the effective and continued application of technology. Furthermore, the general trend towards increased computerization, and the merging of information

SMART QUOTES

The other significant point is that technology, like the evolution of life-forms that spawned it, is inherently an accelerating process.

Ray Kurzweil

and communication technologies, is creating an environment in which technology is becoming the dominant component in most modern enterprises. This centricity is reflected in the levels of spending on IT and although the fallout from the spending associated with Year 2000 still continues to affect chip manufacturers and IT service providers alike, spending on technology continues to take a significant proportion of a company's budget. Global spending on IT is something in the region of $2–3 trillion per annum, and once confidence in the global economy returns, there is nothing to stop this from continuing its upward path, although this is expected to be at a more sedate pace. Indeed worldwide IT services revenue is expected to slow to 2.8 per cent in 2002, but then rise to 7.1 per cent in 2003. So, although not back to double-digit growth, spending on technology is beginning to rise again. There are also those who think that the ultimate end-game for technology is for it to become embedded within ourselves – a desire for man–machine symbiosis which started in the 1950s. A worrying and somewhat depressing prospect, but there are plenty of scientists and technologists who can't wait for this to happen. Ray Kurzweil (1999) describes this as the law of accelerating returns. Whereas the time between the significant astronomical events since the Big Bang has become greater and greater, the time between technological change has got smaller and smaller. If this acceleration is to continue, Moore's Law (which states that the number of transistors that can be housed on a microchip doubles every 18 months – a process which brings with it an increase in power and a corresponding reduction in price, known as the price–performance ratio) will eventually hit the buffers, as new chip technology will unleash more power to the desktop. Researchers are already attempting to replicate the silicon chip molecularly, and this could allow computers to be 100 billion times more efficient than those currently available. Time will tell whether we lose our identity to a machine, but the power of technology and its ability to impact our working lives will continue to affect us, with even greater ferocity. Indeed we witnessed this at the height of the dotcom boom.

SMART VOICES

Supercomputers

Supercomputers are number crunchers that can carry out massive calculations necessary to predict weather, explore space and conduct sophisticated scientific experiments. The latest supercomputer, the Earth Simulator, was recently unveiled by the Japanese. This computer covers the size of four tennis courts, is five times as powerful as IBM's ASCI White supercomputer, took five years to complete, involved over 1,000 people and cost the Japanese government ¥50 billion (£275 million). The Earth Simulator will analyse environmental changes and make predictions about the future climate of the planet. It will achieve this by creating a virtual Earth which will be built using observations from satellites, sea-based monitors and other devices.

(M. Nakamoto, *Financial Times*, 16 Sep. 2002)

Ray Kurzweil

- Millionaire inventor, technologist and prize-winning author.
- Author of *The Age of Intelligent Machines* and *The Age of Spiritual Machines*.
- Asserts that the power of computing will continue to grow exponentially.
- States that in 2029 $1,000 of computing power will have the computational ability of 1,000 human brains (2×10^{19} calculations per second).
- Believes that by 2099 it will be difficult to distinguish between man and computers.

From dotcom to dot bomb

The recent experience with the New Economy is testament to how technology has shifted our thinking and demonstrates how hooked we have all become on the latest technological innovation and the associated business opportunity. The spending fest that accompanied the dotcoms was unbelievable. The fear of being left behind drove perfectly sane businessmen and venture capitalists to invest incredible sums into companies that were destined to crash and burn. It seemed that if you could come up with a crazy-sounding name for an equally crazy-sounding business idea you could have literally millions of dollars thrown at you by hungry venture capitalists, all too greedy to recognize that such enterprises were built on sand. Everyone, it seemed, wanted to believe that the Old Economy was dead. Unfortunately it was this chance of making a fast buck that created the technological bubble that burst in 2000. And like any other bubble, it takes some time

> **Smart things to say**
>
> Beware a gold rush without the gold

to recover, as we are currently witnessing. Some pundits suggest that the current problems are similar to those of the 1930s depression and it will probably take decades for the global economy to recover.

SMART QUOTES

One and a half trillion dollars of market value have been destroyed over the last year in telecoms. BT, for example, has lost 60 per cent of its market value in the last 12 months. There was a lemming effect when these companies rushed to pour billions of dollars of capital into Third Generation Technology and fibre optic networks. As a result there is now an enormous overcapacity that will take years to balance out.

Gary Hamel

The behaviour that culminated in the bursting of the dotcom bubble is of course nothing new, as we have seen this before with other bubbles that burst with similar consequences, including:

- The Tulip Bubble in 1637. When the market for tulips collapsed the price of bulbs had risen 5,900 per cent. Investors lost everything they owned.

- The Southsea Bubble in 1720. A company without any track record or assets was able to convince investors to sell their holdings in worthless Pacific territories at higher and higher prices. When the bubble eventually burst, it took over 100 years for the London Stock Market to recover

Such thinking stems from the belief that a single process, technology or management theory can solve any problem, no matter what its complexity. Such magic bullet solutions are, by their very nature, inherently seductive because they provide senior executives with a straightforward method of resolving a hard-to-crack business problem. Under intense

I'm out of dog food and my cat's box needs new litter. I know what I'll do: I'll order Dog Chow and Fresh Step online from a sock puppet and then I'll watch the dog starve and the cat shit all over the house while I wait for it to be delivered!

Philip Kaplan on Pets.com

pressure to improve operational efficiencies and increase competitive advantage, these managers will grab at anything that, according to those who peddle them, are capable of solving their business problems – often without too much difficulty. This focus on a "one size fits all" approach to management is, like the bubbles that accompany them, nothing new. Originating within the discipline of management theory, it has more recently spilled over into IT – with similar results. Perhaps managers could be forgiven for making the mistake of believing that each new management theory will be the one that provides them with the success they are looking for. But in believing there is a one best way, they feed the theorists and peddlers of such approaches. Moreover, when a particular theory fails to live up to its expectations it is secretly buried, or rejected as being unsuitable. The organization will typically seek out the next magic bullet, with equal fervour and it should be said with equally patchy results. Unfortunately this cycle of adoption, failure and rejection is repeated many times over. This subjects the organization to a constant tirade of change and innovation, the majority of which is pointless. This is particularly bad within IT because the allure of technology. Computer technology can seduce organizations into believing that it is able to solve all of their problems, or as we saw with the botcoms, into believing that the general business disciplines associated with operating any company can be thrown out of the window and replaced by tin-pot ideas. To a large extent, this is fed by books which focus on the power of technology without discussing some of the problems it brings. Unfortunately, this belief in the technological magic bullet can lead organizations to make decisions around major change, or moving into new markets based on technology alone.

> Over the past two decades, bad software has been implicated in plane crashes, road and rail accidents, and malfunctions of medical gear that resulted in death – lending ghoulish new meaning to the term "killer app". Recent glitches have knocked out AT&T's high-speed phone and data networks and interrupted emergency service in New York.
>
> Neil Gross, Marcia Stepanek, Otis Port and John Carey

The headlong rush into the New Economy and the battle between the traditional bricks-and-mortar companies and the Internet start-up organizations led many to believe that the Old Economy was dead. In response, many Old Economy enterprises invested vast sums in technologies that failed to yield any return on investment. This not only applied to retailers, but also those that assumed that digital television would replace analogue and that the world would want to surf the Net on their mobiles. The following are warnings to us all:

- *E-tailers.* Woolworths closed its e-business channel in August 2001 at a cost of £12 million after it failed to attract sufficient customers and lost £15 million. Its Streets online music division forced it to write off £26.7 million after it lost £9 million (Lambeth, 2001).

- *Internet banking.* The Internet banking rush resulted in many banks investing hundreds of millions only to find there were not enough customers to justify their outlay. For example, in late October 2000, Allied Irish Bank became the largest European bank to scale back its online ambitions and plans for an Internet-only bank. It was joined by

Japan's Sanwa Bank, which abandoned its £100 million online bank in favour of adding Internet banking to its other services. These and other banks have realized that there were too many cyber-banks chasing too few customers (Mackintosh, 2000).

- *Digital television.* Two years ago, the UK government hoped the commercial sector could persuade 80 per cent of the British public to pay for their television services, allowing it (the government) to convert the rest. Reality has proved very wide of the mark. Granada and Carlton spent over £900 million on winning just 1.2 million subscribers out of a population of 24 million. The collapse of ITV Digital in 2002 is testament of the failure to address the benefits of technology without considering how attractive the product might be to the consumer (more on this in Chapter 4)

- *Third-generation (3G) mobile telephony.* Over a period of four years telephone companies scrambled over themselves to get a piece of the 3G mobile technology action and licences being offered by governments around the world. Some $4 trillion was spent over this period. As we saw earlier, BT has had to take dramatic action to cope with its enormous debt. They are not alone, as many other companies across Europe are now writing off their investment as realism sets in around the technical viability and likely take-up, which is well short of expectations.

The problems for organizations do not stop here, as even if they have invested wisely, they still have to overcome the hurdle of implementation. This, as we shall see is not an easy task.

Failure to implement technology correctly

As well as falling for the hype of technology, the other issue is that we

How often we imbue technology with magical powers! We think that investments in new machinery or information systems will somehow magically boost productivity, shorten cycle time, cut costs, and accomplish a host of other objectives besides. We believe that products or services – even whole companies – built around new technologies will somehow magically find a market. Most such hopes, of course, are shattered by cold doses of reality. The technology fails to live up to expectations. The dreams built around it vanish with the morning light.

Jonathan Low and Pam Kalafut

have real problems implementing it. This is, of course, nothing new, as our inability to develop software systems that worked was identified as a major issue back in the late 1960s at a 1968 NATO-sponsored conference on the software crisis. At this time software projects were dogged by delays and overruns. It seems that some things never change. This led to the recommendation that companies should engineer software, assuming that software was the same as an engineering project, such as building a bridge, which is of course not the case. Software projects are notorious for their limited success. Most either fail (something in the order of 30 per cent), run late and deliver less than expected (around 50 per cent) and only a small proportion succeed (approximately 20 per cent). There are a multitude of reasons why IT projects fail, and understanding some of these will help to address the balance between success and failure. Such reasons are rarely to do with the technology, as the majority are associated with the nature of organizations, the people employed by them and the problems of not applying sound project management disciplines. In particular, organizations consistently fail to address the change dimension of technology projects, which requires careful attention to how people feel about the new technology and what

SMART
ANSWERS
TO TOUGH
QUESTIONS

it means to their working lives. All too often these are ignored because they are considered to be too difficult to address.

So what's the problem

The issues we face with technology and its management result from the way it has evolved within our organizations over the last fifty to sixty years. Understanding this is critical to smart technology management.

A brief history of time

Initial developments within IT primarily concentrated on the underlying hardware, and were largely laboratory based. Such work took little account of the organizational effect of technological change and innovation. However, once technology had advanced far enough to become useful, organizations were quick to latch onto its possible applications. Unlike the laboratory, where the technology was used in isolation, its introduction into the wider organization proved to be far more problematical.

Computers are everywhere. The versatile silicon chip has found a place in our homes, our schools, our work, and our leisure. We must cope with a flood of new devices, bringing with them both benefits and dangers. Popular books and magazines proclaim that we are witnessing a "Computer revolution", entering a "micro-millennium" in which computers will completely transform our lives.

Terry Winograd and Fernando Flores

Very few commercial IT applications existed prior to the 1950s. Those that did tended to be used by mathematicians or researchers, who were more concerned with the number-crunching abilities of the machines than anything else. The earliest applications of computers within organizations mostly concentrated on formalized and repetitive tasks, such as payroll and accounting. Automating such tasks was attractive because of the advantages associated with the economies of scale. The expensive nature of the systems at this time meant that organizations had to focus their attention on those limited number of areas that lent themselves well to automation, and hence where it was easy to justify the enormous costs.

As the principal repetitive tasks lay within the Finance Division of the organization, it was the natural place to start automating the business. It also allowed them (Finance) to gain valuable experience and expertise within computing and systems development. At that time, the expense of establishing and operating these new systems prevented other departments from purchasing and developing their own – they had to rely on Finance Division's expertise to develop systems for them. And, because Finance controlled all the systems and their associated development activities, this made it difficult for other functions to gain the level of service they required. Hence a significant percentage of the organization was unable to exploit IT to the degree they wanted. In order to diffuse the problem, many organizations decentralized their computing facilities. Unfortunately, this caused more problems than it cured, as it encouraged the proliferation of expensive hardware in areas where computing experience was very limited. It also resulted in the fragmentation of the systems portfolio, and to the duplication of corporate data. As a reaction to this, a centralized data processing unit was established that reported directly to senior management. This unit was designed to provide all departments with an effective, centralized approach to meeting organizational computing needs. During the late 1960s and early 1970s, the development of new operating systems and programming languages resulted in more reliable systems, which, in turn, resulted in a greater demand for systems from the users. By the late 1960s most companies had acquired a large mainframe computer. This was not without its problems, as although businesses started to examine the merits of introducing information systems based on hard financial measures using headcount reductions as their favourite tool, these rarely materialized. Organizations were clearly immature at managing the benefits realization process, and any savings that materialized were largely offset by the increasing costs of managing the systems portfolio – more expert staff and an increasing proportion of activity focused on maintaining the existing systems. And, although this new technology resulted in the transformation of the organization, the development process still concentrated upon technology, and the development cycle was not fast enough to keep up with the typical business cycle.

These problems manifested themselves in an increased dissatisfaction with

KILLER QUESTIONS

How satisfied are
you with the way
technology is
supported?

the centralized data processing department and in the way in which systems were being developed. To tackle this, new development methodologies and engineering approaches were adopted to ensure systems were delivered successfully. By the early 1970s, the mini-computer was becoming more widespread throughout the organization and was effectively superseding the mainframe as the main hardware platform. These were more versatile, required less demanding environmental conditions, and were cheaper than their mainframe equivalent. Furthermore, they had the major advantage of dealing with on-line applications and required fewer professional staff to operate and maintain them. The lower hardware costs meant that smaller user departments were able to purchase their own computers without going over their local budgets. This allowed them to circumvent the internal data-processing department's procurement process, and hence create an invisible wave of IT investment. Further advances in technology during the 1970s and early 1980s, particularly the database, led to a new emphasis on data and information, especially corporate. This was believed to allow universal access, and more importantly, remove the inconsistencies caused by the duplication of data rife within most organizations at that time. In principle, all functions would have access to information belonging to the whole organization, but this global provision of management information failed to materialize for a number of reasons, and principally because of the difficulty in modelling the business – with a constantly changing organization it was impossible to stabilize the data model long enough to create the stable information systems to go with it. This problem was compounded by similar problems with external data.

At about this time, organizations were considering how to integrate their existing IT infrastructure in order to leverage their information needs. This

So what's the problem? It's this: for the first time, the process of technological and business innovation amplifies the normal rhythms of the overall
economy. Funding for innovation now depends on the state of the stock
market and the expected growth of the country's gross domestic product
(GDP). Technology has become synchronized with the ups and downs of the
rest of the economy.

Michael Mandel

system integration activity resulted in the linking of corporate information
systems through networks, databases and associated feeder/receiver systems, and provided clear advantages, not least in data and information
access. But again there were some unforeseen problems. This time associated with the increased complexity, and impact of minor changes made in
one system on another, usually unrelated to the first. In extreme cases, this
could lead to the failure of one system because of a seemingly innocuous
change in another. Such systemic impacts were difficult to locate and
correct, and put a premium on excellent documentation and testing, something that was notoriously poor. During the mid-to-late-1980s, as the
importance and dependence on IT increased, the Board of Directors
became worried and very conscious of having to rely on IT specialists. To
address this, they appointed a manager, to look after this aspect of the business. In the majority of cases they appointed this manager to the board.
Although the appointment of a chief information officer (CIO) was seen as
a strategic move by the chief executive, there appeared to be a problem
with the acceptance of a technologist by the rest of the board. Expected to
integrate IT with the corporate objectives, many CIOs fell short because
they were typically excluded from strategic discussions, and were rarely
involved with setting the direction of the business. In addition, because the
majority of the early CIOs came through the traditional IT career route,
they retained some of their fundamental beliefs about IT – instead of

broadening IT into the mainstream business arena, they concentrated on the operational aspects of managing a major IT function. This culture gap between the business and IT executives at the highest levels was symptomatic of the underlying problem that IT was experiencing with the rest of the organization.

More recently, the boom in outsourcing – where the organization washes its hands of its IT problems by handing it over to a third party – has resulted in some added problems. No longer in control of their IT, organizations are finding that they are having to go through third parties, who really don't care as much as they do. In some instances, the outsourcer cherry-picks the best IT resources for their more lucrative and prestigious clients, leaving the rest to battle with an inferior service. Another problem with outsourcing is that the costs often increase significantly. Having sold the contract on the cheap to make it acceptable to their clients, they then use contractual complexity to add in more and more costs. And finally, there is no guarantee that the projects will be any more successful than before IT was outsourced. Outsourcing may be a growing business, but for a large number of organizations it is probably the worst thing they can do.

What is clear from the foregoing is that technology has the ability to wreak havoc and disrupt. It also has the ability to add immense value. Key to success is smart technology management.

<table>
<tr><td>SMART QUOTES</td><td>Computer software, like the programming field itself, has undergone massive changes in the past few decades. Because hardware and storage tend to be cheap, programmers have a tendency to spend them recklessly, writing "bloatware" – voluminous, inefficient, needlessly complex software.

Bryan Bergeron</td></tr>
</table>

Redressing the balance: smart technology management

Making technology work for the organization rather than the organization working for the technology requires that we change our relationship with it from being one of slave to being one of master. This requires us to:

- Understand how dependent we are on technology and assess the degree to which we are in control (Chapter 1).

- Act like a venture capitalist. In other words, ensuring that every investment in technology is capable of adding value and only selecting those investments that can (Chapter 2).

- Have a total focus on the benefits so that when a technology project completes, we know how it will impact the bottom line (Chapter 3).

- Make sure that we view technology as a product. Product lifecycles count and understanding who the intended audience of the products are should determine how they are built and delivered (Chapter 4).

- Deliver technology projects with care and apply all the right disciplines from project management through to change management (Chapter 5).

- Know how technology will be received, which applies not only to external products, but internal ones too (Chapter 6).

- Select the right approach to manage the technology infrastructure. With choices such as centralization, decentralization and outsourcing, choosing the right one is critical (Chapter 7).

- Make sure that IT is on the agenda at the highest levels in the organization, which means reinventing the CIO – there is no room at the top for a technophile (Chapter 8).

SMART
ANSWERS
TO TOUGH
QUESTIONS

Q. What's so important about technology management? What will it bring to me and my company?

A. Technology is one of the most important drivers of any organization and managing it is crucial for future success. Managing technology wisely by focusing on the upside as well as the downside ensures that you are not seduced by its power. Here are just some of the . . .

Benefits for the Smart individual:

- Increased ability to deal with technological change.
- Real opportunity to drive technological change rather than being driven by it.
- Enhanced awareness and understanding of technology.
- Long-term survival in an increasingly competitive workplace, where technology is increasingly king.

Benefits for the Smart organization:

- Increased ability to manage technology and technology investments.
- Higher success rates in technology projects, with fewer surprises and more benefits.
- Better opportunity to manage technology by selecting the right approach.
- More chance of spotting the next technological innovation and making the right choices about its adoption.
- Long-term survival in an increasingly competitive global economy.

- Keep an eye on the future. Technology changes constantly so it is critical that you do not become blindsided by rapid technological change (Chapter 9).

This book describes what smart technology management means in practice. It is not a trite IT survival guide nor is it one that extols the virtues of technology. What is does is to provide a balanced perspective on how technology can be managed from strategy to delivery. Read on, because smart technology management is an increasingly important skill.

1

How Dependent Are You on Technology?

Nike

Problems in Nike's $400 million overhaul of its supply chain management soft-ware to take advantage of e-commerce resulted in them reporting a reduction in earnings. Nike blamed this entirely on software problems; the first time a company has ever done so.

(A. Heavens, *Financial Times*, 8 Feb. 2001)

As organizations have turned to technology in greater numbers, the levels of dependency have risen sharply. Dependence would not be an issue if the technology worked as expected, but technology is not that predictable. Its complexity makes it systemically unstable and as a result organizations can find themselves literally tied up in knots when it fails. For example:

- Incompatibility between the computers in Scotland's schools and the new Scottish Qualifications Authority's system led to delays and errors in students' results.

- The United Kingdom's Passport Agency hoped that computerizing its offices would reduce the time and unit costs associated with processing passport applications. However, software glitches, and a higher than expected demand for child passports led to such a severe backlog during the summer of 1999, that the Deputy Prime Minister had to intervene to resolve the problem. The cost of the additional measures taken by the Passport Agency to resolve the problems was around £12.6 million, and the unit cost of producing a passport for the year 1999–2000 was expected to be between £15 and £15.50, much higher than the £12 promised in the business case.

- Problems with the UK's Department of Social Security's (now Department for Work and Pensions) national insurance system (NIRS2) resulted in benefit claimants not receiving the money they were entitled to.

- In August 1999, hundreds of customers of UK retailer Tesco were cut off from the supermarket's Internet shopping service for over a week when the software failed. People who had become dependent on the software found that it repeatedly failed after it had been upgraded.

- In August 2002 the low-cost airline Easyjet was forced to abandon its new rostering system and revert back to its old processes because the new system was inadequately tested before it went live and pilots raised concerns over its capabilities (Felsted, 2002).

- After ten years in development the United Kingdom's new air traffic control system has turned the country's airspace into the bottleneck of Europe. The project, which started in 1991, has been plagued by software problems and when it was opened in January 2002 it was five years late and £180 million over budget. The new system has failed to live up to its performance expectations and the United Kingdom is now responsible for more air traffic delays than 30 other countries put together. The most serious problems have been caused by computer bugs and failures which have led to cancellations and delays which have inconvenienced thousands of passengers.

- The State of Florida's Children and Family Services Department child welfare system, which was designed to replace six legacy databases and manual records, has been plagued by politics, poor project management and changes to the system's functionality and architecture. The project started in 1994 and will now come into service in 2005, some five times over budget.

These are just a few of the many examples of both how we look to technology as a way of enhancing our business and what can happen when it fails to live up to expectations. There are of course literally thousands of computer glitches, failures and problems that occur on a daily basis, mainly it has to say whilst we are at work. Computers hang, crash; we lose our work and data. We also lose time because once our computers go down there is little else that we can do because what we do at work often involves computers. If we think more widely we can identify other areas of our lives that require us to depend on technology. Aircraft are increasingly controlled by computers, as are cars. The air traffic control systems on which the busy skies are managed are totally reliant on computer technology. Much of our health systems and retail distribution

> Information technology and other new technologies have provoked profound structural changes in the world economy, and these are concocting unimaginable levels of complexity.
>
> Ian Angell

SMART QUOTES

also relies on technology. Dependence on technology is not a problem *per se*, but when it goes wrong it brings the scale of the dependency into sharp relief.

This of course, is not lost on most of us, as according to a Hays IT survey, organizations do recognize the importance of technology to their success; 91 per cent of the respondents believe that companies who fail to invest in IT will be left behind by those that do, and over half believe that IT is a crucial factor in determining corporate strategy. And yet despite this knowledge many fail to manage their technology resource as well as they should. Instead they make simple errors of judgement with respect to where they need to invest, fail to execute their technology projects professionally and do not consider carefully the strategic importance of technology. This book is designed to address some of these areas and help the smart organization to manage their technology more effectively. This chapter looks at dependency and its consequences. The rest of the book focuses on what to do about it and escribes how to create a culture of smart technology management.

Marks and Spencer

The newly promoted chief executive of the retailer Marks and Spencer has staked his and his company's reputation on technology. Roger Holmes will be investing heavily in new technology that will be embedded within clothing and food packaging. He is looking to the day when chips embedded in food packaging will let staff know when the food has past its sell-by date. He also believes that chips embedded in clothes will tell the purchaser what other clothes match the chosen garment and when being washed on the wrong cycle will warn the user.

(S. Patten, *The Times*, 23 Aug. 2002)

Understanding dependence is key

Organizations need to understand just how dependent they are on technology. Many do not. This leads them to making poor decisions when it comes to deciding on where to invest in new technology. It also allows technology to take on a mind of its own, growing without control and without strategic direction. The problem is that, unlike the changes in technology in the past, such as those associated with the agricultural and industrial revolutions, those associated with modern technology such as IT are less obvious. Indeed computerization tends to creep up on organizations so that, over time they become more dependent upon it without ever realizing. The thing about technology is that once you become dependent on it you have no choice but to maintain that dependency – you cannot undo what is already done. If we know how dependent we are on technology we should be able to manage it more effectively, and through this careful management reduce some of the risks we face. Indeed, the Year 2000 problem demonstrated just how dependent we all were. As the millennium drew near organizations spent billions updating their IT systems, facility management systems and infrastructures to ensure they could cope with the change in date from 1999 to 2000. Although the date change passed with limited problems, this was the first time that there was a collective understanding of just how dependent we were on technology.

Answering the following questions will allow you to test your likely level of dependency and your knowledge of how technology might drive your organization. As we saw at the turn of the millennium, the only direct measure of how dependent we actually are is the belief that we are heading for technological meltdown. Only then do we take a

KILLER QUESTIONS
Do you know how
dependent you
are on technology?

long hard look at our critical systems. I believe we can be smarter than this by shifting from this disaster-based, reactive mentality to one that is more forward thinking and proactive. Only then will we ensure we do not repeat the Year 2000 approach to managing technology.

Lauren Weiner

- Author of *Digital Woes*.
- Identified the dangers of IT dependency.
- Recognized thirteen digital woes — when things go wrong with computer technology:

1. Tiny errors can have large effects
2. Thorough testing takes too long
3. Developing software is not the easiest way to make money
4. Even a careful process can leave a problem
5. Sometimes the upgrade is late
6. We risk our reputations
7. We risk financial disaster
8. We risk democracy
9. We risk death
10. We risk the earth's ability to sustain life
11. We may not gain much
12. We may solve the wrong problem
13. Life is unpredictable

When answering the questions, select one option only. I have not scored these because you will be able to judge your own levels of dependency as you answer each question. I have, however provided some commentary beneath each. Assessing how dependent you are on technology is not a scientific exercise, more of a judgement, as you can't necessarily measure dependency directly (apart from question 4). However, once you have answered the following questions you will have some understanding of how much you may (or may not) depend on technology.

1. Do you know how much your organization spends on technology?

(a) Yes, precisely.

(b) Yes, within a reasonable tolerance

(c) No, not without some research.

(d) No, I haven't got a clue.

The level of spending on IT is a surrogate measure of dependency. The more you spend, the higher the levels of dependency. The levels of spending on IT have, until recently continued to climb year on year, usually in double digits. Even though the bursting of the dotcom bubble and the excess of Year 2000 spending have depressed the chip manufacturers and IT integrators, it is still necessary to invest in IT. Indeed, many companies have little choice but to continue to spend in order to meet the demands of more demanding customers and the need to eke out operational efficiencies through the application of technology. This last point is particularly relevant during periods of economic uncertainty. Although global IT spend is huge, it masks considerable variations in spend across individual organizations and sectors, as it will vary according to the size and nature of the business. For example, global investment backs spend significantly more on their IT than retailers because they depend on the accurate flow of financial information around the globe. This can only be achieved through a complex web of systems that are able to feed information to the traders, assess risk, settle trades and account for the money flowing between the bank, its counterparts and clients. As a result individual investment banks can spend more than £1 billion per annum on IT. Conversely, a retailer's IT is much simpler because it focuses on such things as inventory management, point of sale systems warehousing and distribution.

Global foreign exchange settlement system

On 9 September 2002, after five years of talks and development, a global settlement system for the $2,000 billion a day foreign exchange market was launched. The continuous linked system (CLS) which joins together seven central banks and the bulk of the world's leading trading banks replaces the existing two-day settlement with a five-hour period that covers the complete process of funding, settlement and payment.

(A. Skorecki, Financial Times, 9 Sep. 2002)

It is important to know how much you spend on IT not only because it indicates how dependent you might be, but also for its effective management. This can be assessed in a number of ways, with spend as a percentage of turnover being one of the best. Also, when it comes to spending, it is important to recognize that there is a significant amount that is hidden from view. A lot of IT investments are absorbed into departmental and functional budgets especially if it is decentralized. It is also believed that between 4 and 10 per cent of end users' time is spent on helping their colleagues solve their software problems. This hidden time is believed to cost something in the region of $23,500 per personal computer per year.

2. Do you know what value your technology adds to your business?

(a) Yes.

(b) No, not without further analysis.

(c) Not at all.

This is as critical as the first question. Many organizations invest in technology hoping to derive some benefit from it. Most fail because there is no rigour in assessing or tracking the benefits. As the levels of dependency increase, it becomes harder to assess where the benefits really lie or where the value comes from. This is because much of the automation and radical change that followed the early computerization of work has been completed, leaving very few big ticket automation opportunities left. That said, technology investments are increasingly complex and often involve replacing legacy systems or introducing enterprise-wide applications. These are expensive undertakings which ought to be providing some value to the business. Failing to measure the value from technology often leads the organization to continue to invest in other technologies in the hope that they will provide the value that previous investments have not. This, unfortunately is the wrong strategy.

CityReach International

CityReach International, the owner of eight Internet data centres in Europe, went into administration in August 2001, less than a year after it raised $155 million in funding. The company blamed poor take-up of its web hosting and co-location services for large companies. The failure was due to too many data centre service companies chasing too few customers. A very similar story to the Internet banks. The company had spent $180 million opening centres in London, Amsterdam, Budapest, Stockholm and Paris, but to no avail.

(C. Grande, Financial Times, 29 Aug. 2001)

SMART VOICES

3. Can you identify your core IT systems?

(a) Yes.

(b) No.

Core systems are those that the organization depends on the most. Without these the business would be severely disrupted, and if they were inoperable for more than a short period the company could go out of business. For example, when the Stock Exchange system goes down the whole of the UK's financial markets comes to a standstill. When the air traffic control systems fail, no planes can take off. For other organizations it is their supply chain or customer relationship management systems. The nature and number of core systems will vary from organization to organization – some are reliant on one or two, others on a large number. The shift to major enterprise resource planning systems such as SAP can create an over reliance on a single system, which increases the risk of enterprise-wide disruption. It is essential that you understand which systems you depend on the most and ensure suitable back-up is available. If you don't know, find out. In general, core systems have to be well developed and well maintained. The other issue that organizations now face is the systemic risks associated with a failure in one core system affecting another. With major systems feeding data to one another, the danger of one failure affecting other systems and the entire business is increasingly real.

4. If your technology failed how long would it be before your business would suffer?

(a) Weeks.

(b) Days.

(c) Hours.

SMART
ANSWERS
TO TOUGH
QUESTIONS

This is a true measure of dependency, but one you cannot afford to assess in real time. With a greater dependency comes an increase in the financial risks that a failure in a core system can bring (see Smart voices and the Bank of New York). As we saw with the Year 2000 date change, organizations (in the main) were unwilling to take the risk of technological meltdown and took expensive precautions to prevent it. They believed that they could not survive long without their IT systems and infrastructures. How long an organization can survive after a computer crash will, of course, vary considerably. For example, the global finance system would not last very long at all, probably a matter of hours and

Bank of New York

On 20 November 1985, a bug cost the Bank of New York $5 million when the software used to track government securities transactions from the Federal Reserve suddenly began to write new information onto the old. When the software bug hit the system, it was impossible for the bank to identify who owed what, and at the close of business on 20 November, it was $32 billion overdrawn with the Federal Reserve. The software error was located and corrected in just two days, but at a cost of $5 million – to cover short-term interest on the $32 billion loan.

(T. Forester and P. Morrison, *Computer Ethics*, 1994)

SMART VOICES

maybe a day or two. Others could cope for a lot longer, but as time goes by and as organizations continue to replace manual activity with computer-based processes, weeks will eventually become days and perhaps even hours. As the time reduces, the importance of having suitable contingency and business continuity plans in place becomes more critical. For example, the recovery of the New York Stock Exchange following the attacks on the World Trade Centre on 11 September 2001 demonstrates how important such plans are. The Stock Exchange was up and running within a few days following the attacks and the desire of the terrorists to destroy what they believed to be the heart of Western capitalism failed. Ironically, the corporate scandals of Enron, WorldCom, Tyco and the many others has served to do more damage than the terrorists hoped for.

5. Do you automatically turn to technology when there is a business problem to solve?

(a) Never, I always consider the wider options.

(b) Sometimes.

(c) Always.

SMART QUOTES

Technocentricity is a very specific form of corporate narcissism. The love that blinds in technocentricity is the belief that new technologies, by definition, always provide better deals than old technologies.

Eileen Shapiro

This is an increasingly important issue. Too many organizations turn to technology without fully assessing the costs, benefits and long-term implications. We should recognize that problems are rarely solved with technology alone. Certainly a combination of technology, process change and people makes for more effective change. But most organizations tend to focus on technology before considering the wider options. A lot of organizational change can be achieved through the effective management of people, their talent and their careers. Indeed, the recent interest in talent management is testament to this. Too often organizations believe that technology is capable of solving any problem and are willing to throw good money after bad in order to do so. As we know from experience, without due care and attention, money unwisely invested in technology costs the organization dear. It is far better to consider the problem in hand on a much wider footing that encapsulates the people, process and organizational design elements as well as the technological. In this way a better solution can be established that applies technology more effectively. Thus if you have answered (c) to this question you would be wise to consider your next business problem more

General Motors

In the early 1980s, General Motors embarked upon an enormous investment in automation in its automotive production plants (Wiener, 1994). In 1985 it opened its showcase factory, which boasted 50 automatic guided vehicles and 260 robots. Almost a year later, however, performance of the plant was significantly lower than expected – it was only capable of producing half the number of cars per day it was expected to. The production lines ground to a halt with regular frequency, while the technicians tried frantically to debug the software. Even when the robots did work, they tended to smash cars, fit the wrong equipment and even dismantle each other. It later transpired that General Motors' problems lay not with its production processes, but with the way it treated its employees – it was a solution to the wrong problem. This meant that they had to revisit their approach to managing their human resources – which they had assumed, quite wrongly, was not the problem – at an equally enormous expense.

carefully. Part of the issue resides in the limited knowledge and understanding that most people have about what technology can and cannot do. Charles Wang, chief executive officer of Computer Associates, terms the use of such techno-speak the ignorance lobby, because there are numerous consultants, analysts, associations and journalists who want to reinforce the high levels of technical ignorance within the general populace. All, he suggests have a stake in the continued ignorance of information technology, as this allows each to cultivate their business by peddling the latest technology, designed to solve the latest business problem. The focus on technology leads organizations to invest without thinking, following what their competitors have done or taking the advice of IT suppliers at face value. Ultimately, every organization should be responding to this question by choosing (a). If this were so, every enterprise would be smart at managing their technology. Unfortunately, this is far from the case.

6. Do you feel that you have no choice when a technology supplier suggests that it is time to upgrade your systems?

(a) Always.

(b) Sometimes.

(c) Never.

SMART QUOTES

The constant market pressure to offer computers with more and better features, and therefore to provide a reason to purchase another computer, even when a customer's existing machine performs adequately, results in a continuous stream of new and "improved" operating systems. New computer buyers have little choice in the matter . . .

Bryan Bergeron

Most technology has a degree of inbuilt obsolescence to it. We come to expect that our home appliances and cars gradually wear out. But when it comes to software we expect it to function perfectly every time. This is of course far from the truth. Our experience with software is tainted by the need to constantly upgrade. In the main this is driven by the vendors updating their software to address bugs, or to increase functionality. As software is updated, it typically involves an increase in the number of features it provides. For example, the number of commands in Microsoft Word increased from 311 in 1992, to 1033 in 1997. If the user wished to master this later version, it would take a lot longer than it had with the earlier one. In addition, the power and memory required to run this later version is significantly higher than that required to run the former. Therefore any software upgrade – at least when associated with the desktop – can often require simultaneous hardware upgrades. As a result, organizations find themselves in a bind. Do they standardize on a particular version of the software, recognizing that one day they will have to upgrade when the supplier withdraws their support, or do they follow the supplier's lead and upgrade whenever the latest version of the software is out? This is a very difficult issue to address.

The other problem is that once your staff have mastered a particular system, and particularly the work-arounds required to get over the various imperfections and bugs, there is an overhead associated with any upgrade. The more radical the change in the software's look and feel, the greater the training and learning overhead. This costs companies dear as their productivity dips as they get to grips with the new system. The issue is that most of this is out of the control of the organization because software suppliers will deliver updates to their soft-

KILLER QUESTIONS

Are you getting value out of your suppliers?

ware to correct bugs and flaws which, if the organization is to have the advantage of, they must upgrade or apply the software patch. In addition, most suppliers will stop supporting old versions of their software or operating system resulting in a mandatory upgrade for the business. I would be very surprised if anyone answered (a) to this question, as even the largest of corporates have limited choice when it comes to upgrades.

SMART QUOTES

The situation hasn't always been so dire. There was a time, in the 1970s, when companies could rely on nearly bulletproof software, supplied by mainframe computer companies such as IBM and Sperry. Not only was the code dependable, but the hardware environment was relatively homogeneous. Less complexity meant fewer glitches. Then came computer "downsizing" and the so-called client–server revolution, in which thousands of businesses shifted operations from mainframes to distributed networks of workstations and PCs. This model spelled the demise of insulated, bug-free software and left corporations exposed to the fast-and-dirty culture of PC software.

Neil Gross, Marcia Stepanek, Otis Port and John Carey

7. Do you believe that your company can compete without the use of technology?

(a) Yes.

(b) No.

(c) Not sure.

This question requires some serious thought. Although we may automatically answer "no" to this question, believing that technology is the defining factor in an organization's success, there are other things that are probably far more important. Consider the war for talent. Companies rise and fall based upon their human capital, and as the

Information Age takes hold, the need for more versatile, intelligent and experienced employees will increase. Unfortunately with a declining population and global competition, most organizations are finding it difficult to recruit and retain their most talented employees. No amount of technology will help (as we saw with General Motors). Furthermore, survey after survey points to the competitive advantage that talented individuals can provide. Another factor associated with competitive advantage is organizational culture. Peters and Waterman, the McKinsey consultants who wrote *In Search of Excellence*, believed that an organization's culture was a strong determinant in their success. Similar conclusions have been drawn by others. So it seems that beating the competition can be achieved more readily through softer factors such as people and culture than through technology. Also if you consider that many organizations have installed systems such as Enterprise Resource Planning and Customer Relationship Management, all of which provide similar functionality, it should be clear that technology alone does not provide competitive advantage. The only caveat to this is using technology to gain first-mover advantage. Ultimately the success of the organization will depend on a variety of factors, which include the soft as well as the hard. Naturally technology will have its part to play, but it is not the only factor.

8. Does your organization lack the technology skills required to exploit your existing technology and develop the new?

(a) Yes, definitely.

(b) No, I am not absolutely sure.

(c) Definitely not, we have enough of the right resources.

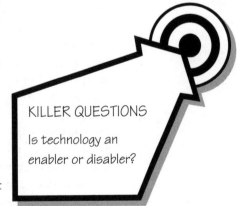

KILLER QUESTIONS

Is technology an enabler or disabler?

The war for talent is particularly acute within the technological domain. Shortages of staff with the requisite technical skills and experience are a problem for most organizations. Few companies have all the technical resources, they need and as more staff are consumed by the maintenance activities needed for existing systems, less are available to develop the systems of the future. In the recent past, organizations have been desperate for technology experts, even turning to the long-term unemployed for the raw talent they need. Indeed, the skills shortage has not been lost on government. For example, the late 1990s skills crisis in the United Kingdom's IT community prompted the government to establish

Smart things to say about technology management

Companies must be nimble not monolithic. Innovative and flexible, not predictable or slow to react to change. ERP systems and the enforced compromises that the technology imposes on the company for a smoother implementation, renders the company inflexible to change.

a working party to tackle the problem, and in particular to try and make the profession an exciting place to be for the country's brightest graduates. This action followed hot on the heels of a report which claimed that high-flying graduates were shunning the IT profession because they believed it offered limited career opportunities, and little in the way of interpersonal and management development, all of which are vital components of a stimulating and varied career. When it comes to dealing with the problem, organizations have turned to outsourcers, consultants and software suppliers in greater numbers to plug the gaps. The real problem, however, lies in the continuous stream of new technologies, systems and operating environments, all of which require deep technology skills and expertise. Ironically, it is difficult for the technology practitioners to keep track of the rapid advances, numerous product

The National Health Service

Alan Millburn, the Labour Health Minister, is seeking to double the amount of money spent on IT in the UK's health service. This would bring the annual budget to £2.2 billion. The task ahead is, as a recent job advertisement for a new director-general of IT is Herculean, especially as recent attempts at implementing state-of-the-art IT have failed. Millburn is hoping to use technology to bring the UK's health service in line with that of the US. The new money will be spent on electronic patient records, digital prescriptions, booked admissions and other advances. When only 5 per cent of National Health Service Trusts have electronic patient records, it's no wonder the task is considered so great. The history of large government projects is poor, so this might turn out to be a bridge too far.

launches and technical literature associated with IT. This creates problems when the organization wishes to implement the latest technology; they just don't have the skills. Moreover, they need to retain the legacy skills in order to keep the business running. As a result everyone finds themselves in a bind. The organization can't find the technical skills it needs, the technologists don't want to work on the legacy systems and everyone lurches from one new technology to the next. The only way to resolve this is to attempt to stabilize on a small number of technologies and ensure these work very well. This is, however, a very tall order as we saw in question 6.

9. *Do you believe you could conduct your work without the use of technology?*

(a) Yes, definitely.

(b) Not entirely.

(c) Definitely not.

I believe that we should all answer (c) to this question. If we are honest, none of us could work without technology and, as the future generations grow up with it, they are unlikely to know anything else. As we saw earlier, when organizations implement disaster recovery and business continuity plans, the degree to which we rely on technology is brought into stark relief. What it also does is to force organizations and the people within them to consider whether they really need their technology. We could live without it for a short while but most people feel naked without their laptops and other systems that allow them to complete their daily work. The reason for this is quite simple. Over the past fifty years, technology has replaced a large proportion of manual activities that we have been used to. Consider the simple activity of writing a document. In the past you would draft it by hand, send it to the typing pool and it would reappear a day or so later. You would then make any corrections send it back to the typing pool and the job would be complete. Now, with no typing pools we all write our own documents on our laptops or PCs. This not only takes longer because we revise them many times over, but it means that should our word processing software or laptop fail, we have no other means of producing the document because the old process for producing documents has long disappeared.

Although trivial, this example reflects what has changed. We are no longer capable of executing our work without technology because most of the business processes have been subsumed within the technology we use. This has led to the removal of the traditional organizational support mechanisms, like typing pools. Most of the significant business processes are now either managed or controlled by technology or at the very least require a heavy doses of technology to be effectively completed.

10. Do you know how much it costs you to maintain your systems?

(a) Yes, we track our costs.

(b) Not sure.

(c) No.

Technology management does not stop after implementation, as there is an ongoing cost that has to be accounted for. This is often lost on organizations as they absorb the maintenance of their technology within their operational budgets. It is important, however, to consider these costs more carefully and certainly in light of the value this expenditure brings to the business. For example, where systems support the sale of a product it is useful to weigh up the product's revenue against the internal support costs, as sometimes this could be a bit of a shock. For example, a number of years ago I inherited the maintenance of a system that had been implemented to develop and maintain a new product. By the time I inherited the system, it was some months after implementation, and the organization was spending something in the region of £200,000 per annum maintaining it (approximately four staff). I attended a product review meeting shortly after taking it on, and learnt that, having spent approximately £1,000,000 on the system and product development activity, only one customer had signed up to the product. Thus, for an initial investment of £1,000,000 and an ongoing maintenance bill of £200,000, the organization was only gaining some £40,000 in annual revenue. As new systems are developed more and more staff become involved in maintenance activities rather than developing the new technologies that will support the business in the future. Tracking these costs carefully and understanding what value they bring is essential.

This chapter has focused on helping you understand the degree to which you and the organization in which you work are dependent on technology. There is little point bemoaning the high levels of dependence because this will not change and if anything is likely to continue to increase. Assessing dependency helps to bring organizations out of the bind they find themselves in and forces them to recognize the need to become more efficient and effective at how they manage their technology. It also helps them to ensure that they are managing technology, not the other way around. This is the focus of the next six chapters. In the end technology is too important to leave it in the hands of the technologists. Technology management is business management – the two can no longer be separated.

2

Smart Thinking I – Act Like a Venture Capitalist

Beyond any doubt, venture capital is the fastest-growing part of the finance system. In 1999, venture capital firms dispersed $48 billion to new start-ups. In the first quarter of 2000, venture capital funding was running at roughly a $90 billion annual rate.

Michael Mandel

SMART QUOTES

Venture capitalists were literally falling over themselves at the height of the dotcom boom. Any idea, no matter how crazy, was able to secure start-up funding in the hope that the initial public offering (IPO) would make huge returns. But despite the ludicrous nature of this, there are some general lessons we can learn from venture capitalists. If those responsible for technology management, which I believe is the entire board of directors, were to adopt some of the principles associated with investing in a new venture, they might be more successful in their technology investments. After all, the purpose behind venture capital is to provide sufficient money to allow a new technology to get off the ground. This, coupled with careful management and a willingness to pull the plug when the idea looks as though it is going to fail, ensures money is appropriately spent.

By March 9, 2000, 378 Internet companies were publicly traded, with a collective market capitalization of $1.5 trillion — amazing considering this was supported by only $40 billion in total annual sales; most of which was concentrated in the hands of a few companies such as Qwest, AOL and Amazon.com. And, most incredibly, 87 percent of those 378 Internet companies had yet to even show a quarterly report . . . Between Spring 2000 and July 2001, 300 Internet companies laid-off a total of 31,000 employees. And 103 dot.com companies have closed down altogether. By December 22, 2000, the total market capitalization of public Internet companies had plummeted by 75 percent — meaning over a trillion dollars of value had evaporated in under one year.

Jim Harris

Lessons from the dotcoms

Since the demise of the dotcoms there has been plenty of advice coming from the business gurus who were previously persuading the same businesses to join in the gold rush that was the New Economy. Although plenty of shirts were lost in the process, we can draw some important lessons from the dotcoms and the failed investments in electronic commerce so that we don't make the same mistakes as before. These lessons are:

1. Technology is highly disruptive both in general and particularly to the business status quo. Although nothing new, the more we come to rely on technology, the more we should expect disruption. The dotcom boom shook up the existing business models based upon property and tangible assets. It forced organizations to wake up to many things, including the war for talent (in essence their intangible assets), the competition from new business start-ups that could compete almost immediately and the importance of the Internet as a channel to market. The lesson that this implied was that you cannot ignore new technology and in fact, you must track it and assess its implications. More on this in Chapter 9.

2. Technology investments are inherently risky. This means that every project has to be handled with care. Betting the company on a new technology and then failing to develop or test it properly can be fatal. This implies that organizations must become more professional at managing the introduction of new technology. Some of the specifics of this are discussed in Chapter 5

3. Technology has the ability to soak up vast amounts of money. Without careful management organizations can end up investing literally hundreds of millions in a venture that yields no value. The invisible nature of technology means that it is very difficult to monitor its development. It is also difficult to know whether it will work when complete. This makes the financial management of technology investment even more critical.

KILLER QUESTIONS

How many of your technology investments are money sinks?

4. Technology on its own will not create value. Without developing sound business models for its exploitation, any investment will be wasted. Furthermore, without considering the human dimensions of how it will be used and accepted, the technology will be destined to lie on a shelf. The critical role of the reception strategy is covered in Chapter 7.

5. Technology failure is generally more visible because it increasingly touches the customer. For example, the failure of the Inland Revenue's online tax system to prevent people from seeing other taxpayers' data in May 2002 resulted in a 32-day suspension of its Internet self-assessment service. Although clearly embarrassing, the failure has undermined people's willingness to sign up to the service.

In better times, it wasn't so difficult for venture capitalists. In fact the odds could be laughable. Find a private technology company, throw some money at it, then take it public. Ten-to-one you'd make out like a bandit.

Peter Henig

A brief history of venture capitalism[1]

Venture capital has increased to the point where it rivals research and development (R&D) as a source of funding for innovation. In the first quarter of 2000 it equalled fully one-third of all money spent on R&D, compared to an average of 3 per cent in the 1980s.

Although venture capitalists were very prominent during the dotcom

[1] For a detailed review of venture capitalism, see Gompers and Lerner (1999).

The railway industry

There are a lot of parallels between the railway industry of the nineteenth century and the dotcoms of the twentieth. Both involved huge amounts of speculative investment and both experienced a major crash (1845 for the railways and 2000 for the dotcoms). But, we should take note that even those companies that were to become the dominant players in the railway industry once the markets recovered still suffered when the bubble burst. There are parallels too. Both gave rise to start-ups, large and small, and both resulted in a shift in management thinking, required to drive profitability in the new technology. It's probably too early to write off the dotcoms and there is some evidence that they are beginning to rise out of the ashes.

boom, they actually represent an important and long-standing source of financing in all major economies. Indeed, venture capital is beginning to rival research as a means of bringing new ideas to market. In the past when entrepreneurs had ideas that they could not fund themselves, they had very few alternatives but go to banks, or their equivalent in pre-banking times, such as moneylenders. However without any tangible assets on which to secure a loan, many were left high and dry. This is where the venture capitalist came in. These were people who were willing to invest in high-risk, high-return ventures. As an industry, venture capitalism is relatively young. The first venture capital firm did not appear until immediately after the Second World War. The firm, American Research and Development, funded some of the well-known names in the technology industry including the Digital Equipment Company. Funding by venture capitalists grew significantly over the period 1946–1995 when it started to rise rapidly to cope with the emergence of the dotcoms and technology start-up companies. After the boom turned to bust, venture capitalists became a lot more wary of what they were willing to invest in. That said, they continue to commit to those ideas that will yield value including communications, computers, biotechnology, electronics and energy. There is also strong evidence that the continued weakness in the global economy and the poor state of the world's stock exchanges is resulting in an increasing number of entrepreneurs turning to venture capitalists rather than the banks for support.

Benefits of thinking like a venture capitalist[2]

> Thomas Edison was a great inventor but a poor businessman. Consider the phonograph. Edison invented it, he had better technology than his competitors, and he did a sensible, logical analysis of the business. Nonetheless, he built a technology-centered phonograph that failed to take into account his customer's needs. In the end, his several companies proved irrelevant and bankrupt.
>
> Donald Norman

This quote about Edison sums up some of the problems with technology. For example, there is a real issue with the way technology overrides any detailed thinking about the customer (more on this in Chapter 5). The issue we will be dealing with in this chapter is the ability to back winners and manage the financial aspects of technology. The smart organization knows that technology has the capability of becoming a money sink in which good money after bad is thrown on a failing product or project. They also know that thinking like a venture capitalist helps them to avoid some of the financial pitfalls.

[2]See Mandel (2000, pp. 24–31).

There are four benefits that thinking like a venture capitalist will bring to an organization:

1. Profit-making

Venture capitalists are ruthless in their pursuit of profit. Nothing else matters. Money will only ever be directed to those investments that provide the highest return. Naturally an organization has to invest in many different things, and even when it comes to technology, there is a need to spend on infrastructure. However, the basic principle of seeking out profits is sound and not just for those technology investments that will be sold on the open market. Adopting the same principle for internal technology investments is also important because it is these that drive operational efficiencies, innovation and change. The simple reason why this attitude is valuable is because of the increasing size of investment that is required. When organizations invest vast sums in an enterprise-wide application, they need to be sure that it is going to deliver.

2. Diversification

Venture capitalists by their very nature have to seek out as many opportunities as possible. The diversification of investment portfolio allows them to hedge against those projects that will ultimately fail. Their approach recognizes that not every investment will succeed, and the best way to hedge against failure is to spread their bets. Although organizations do not have the ability to widen their investments because of the need to fund their business as usual activities, they do have the ability to extend their technology investments through such things as research and development and incuba-

KILLER QUESTIONS

How do you view failure –
as a blessing
or a curse?

tors. They can also hedge against those projects that will ultimately fail. Diversification also helps organizations to get over the inherent difficulties associated with innovation. It is well known that the majority of companies struggle to innovate for a variety of reasons. Careful diversification can help

3. Weeding

The ruthless focus on seeking profit drives the venture capitalist to weed out those investments that will not provide the returns they seek. This is achieved through a staged approach to funding. Typically money is provided to develop the idea to IPO, in essence seeing if it will make any money. Further funding is usually provided once the company has gone public. This approach not only limits the financial risk of the venture capitalists, it also provides a powerful incentive to those involved with the start-up to make it a success. The most important benefit that weeding provides, however, is the unemotional way it deals with failure. Failure is part of the equation and instead of becoming emotionally attached to a particular venture, the investors will walk away rather

SMART VOICES

The Libra project

The Libra project is the UK government's initiative to speed up the criminal justice system. The project, which started in 1998, was expected to cost £183 million. However, it soon became clear that the project's costs had been grossly underestimated, as its price shot up to £319 million. Further price increases by the supplier, Fujitsu, have been rejected and the software agreement has been scrapped. The Lord Chancellor's Department justified its decision on the grounds that cheaper and better software was available elsewhere. The UK taxpayer will, however, still have to pay £232 million for the hardware, which has already been installed.

than allow it to become a money sink. Organizations can learn a lot from this, as typically everything the venture capitalist does, the organization does not. If we accept that that not every technology project will succeed, we need to become better at dealing with failure. This means avoiding the problems associated with over commitment (see Chapter 6).

4. Management

The venture capitalist approach also involves looking after their investment by providing access to management ability. It usually includes stepping in with a strong management team when required. This behaviour once again stems from the ruthless focus on profit and the unemotional nature of the venture capitalist; they will do everything they can to protect their investment. Clearly organizations are a little different from a venture capitalist, but they too should take a keen interest in the management of their technology investments. All too often a poorly skilled project manager is placed at the helm and management washes their hands of the project once it has started. Every technology project needs to be managed and senior management should be keen for it to succeed, even if it means replacing those in charge of it.

Recognizing the benefits of acting like a venture capitalist is essential for smart technology management because it guards against the many pitfalls associated with investing in technology.

Making sound investments

The real purpose behind effective venture capitalism is that it is designed to make sound investments. We should of course remember that sound investments not only equate to success; it also means pulling the plug on those that are not going to add any long-term value. Such

> **Red Herring magazine**
> - Technology magazine.
> - Provides a barometer on the technology markets, what's new and what will happen in the future.
> - Gives an honest view of what works and what is a red herring.

investments can still be valuable because they help to inform decisions and prevent organizations from investing in unsuitable products and technologies. Although most organizations do not need venture capital, they should be seeking to secure the benefits that thinking like a venture capitalist brings. They should also be willing to follow a typical route through any venture, namely:

- Identify potential investments.

- Assess these investments and select those with the greatest chance of success.

- Stage the funding based on progress.

- Shut down any investment, that based upon progress or new information is no longer viable.

- Exit the investment and secure the benefits.

Most organizations tend to be poor at some or all of these steps and a significant part of technology management is associated with making sure that each of the above steps is effectively managed. They can be summed up as – invest wisely, spend wisely and secure the benefits. The benefit side of the equation is dealt with in Chapters 4 and 7. Spotting the potential investment areas is covered in Chapter 9 as this is strongly linked to setting strategy. This chapter deals with appraising the investment and staging the funding. In many respects the philosophy behind venture capitalism runs throughout the book and is a central theme to managing technology.

Starting out

Every technology investment requires a sound understanding of its financial requirements. To do this requires that the business has an appropriate investment appraisal mechanisms in place. Investing in technology is rarely easy and the simple techniques that we have come to rely on for other types of capital expenditure are not always applicable. The point of understanding what the investment is likely to cost and what sort of return can be expected from it is to allow the board of

SMART
PEOPLE
TO HAVE
ON YOUR
SIDE

Paul Nutt

- Professor of Management Sciences and Public Policy and Management in the Fisher College of Business at Ohio State University.
- Author of numerous books, including *Why Decisions Fail*.
- Believes that the root causes of major failures and bad decisions lie in three blunders:
  1. *Failure-prone practices.* Nutt believes that two out of every three decisions use error-prone practices and decision-makers seem to be oblivious to them.
  2. *Premature commitments.* Decision-makers will select the first idea that comes into their mind and then spend years trying to make them work.
  3. *Wrong-headed investments.* Too much time is spent on evaluating the upside of an investment and not enough considering the risks or benefits.

directors to decide whether they are willing to spend the money on this or something else. Moreover, making the right investment decisions should be of interest to shareholders and other external investors as failure to deliver on the promises can lead to drops in share prices such as that which followed the realization that BT's purchase of 3G licences were more of a millstone than a benefit.

One way of assessing the investment is to compare the ease of implementation (which is a surrogate indication of costs and complexity) against likely return as this helps to prioritize competing investments (Figure 2.1). The quadrants are:

- *Value accelerators* (high value and simple to implement). These are the low-hanging fruit that are well worth investing in because a good return can be secured relatively easily.

- *Strategic* (high value but difficult to implement). These are invest-

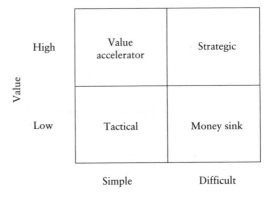

Ease of implementation

Figure 2.1 Assessing investments.

ments that are complex, expensive and time consuming. They are rarely implemented rapidly and they are often "bet the company" type investments that transform the business and can drive or change markets. They are well worth investing in because of the impact they can have but more than any other they require careful management and it is important to ensure they do not fall into the next category.

- *Money sinks*. Many technology investments end up in this category. They turn out to be low value and difficult to implement. Very often projects are launched in a hail of glory, with great hopes and high expectations. Unfortunately many turn out to be money sinks in which good money is thrown after bad. However because of bad decision making (see Smart People to Have on Your Side: John Nutt) these are never spotted until they are well under way, which then makes it very difficult to stop them (see Chapter 6, and guarding against the Mastermind "I've started so I'll finish" project).

- *Tactical*. These are projects that are necessary to satisfy a short-term need which may only provide limited benefits. However because of their relationship to a specific issue or to other long-term strategic projects, they are worth investing in. The key thing is to remember is that you cannot have too many as this would suggest there is no strategic direction or effective management of technology. Ultimately a healthy mix of tactical and strategic projects ensures an appropriate focus on the short and long term.

Another categorization of technology investments, and especially those that are related to IT is shown in Table 2.1.

Staging the funding

Venture capitalists stage their funding. The reason for this is quite

Table 2.1 IT investment types

Investment category	Description
Mandatory	Typically externally driven, for example through regulatory or political pressure/legislation. Decisions in such instances tend to be confined to choosing a design which meets these externally imposed requirements, whilst at the same time minimizing the costs to the organization.
Automation	Technology designed to replace existing methods and/or processes in order to reduce costs. They may provide little in the way of business innovation and may, apart from the reduction in headcount, have only a limited impact on the profitability of the business.
Direct value added	Technologies which are designed to add direct value through a combination of cost reduction and leveraging value through innovation. Such projects are designed to make significant impacts on the organization's effectiveness and efficiency.
Management information and decision support systems	Technologies that provide information for planning, control and decision making. These are usually focused at senior and middle management, and are aimed at making general improvements in their efficiency.
Infrastructure	Technologies that provide a general capability but may not be targeted at any specific functional area. These are one of the most difficult types of project to gain commitment and funding for, as it is hard to demonstrate a direct positive return on the investment. However, they do provide the foundation upon which further applications and investments can be made.

straightforward: they want to manage their risks and to protect – as much as they can – their investment. If we remember that they only invest in order to make a healthy return, it seems sensible to stage the money they provide to the entrepreneur. In a similar vein organizations

Farbey, Land and Targett

- Authors of *How to Assess your IT Investment*.

- Discuss in detail the importance of marrying the method used to evaluate a technology project to the type of IT investment.

- Recommend the use of an approach which assesses the technology project from the dual perspectives of the role which IT is to adopt – which includes the types of benefit, the relationship of the project to the business and its certainty of impact, and the associated evaluation constraints – which includes the timing of the evaluations, the nature of the decision making process, the nature of the system, and the industry situation.

- The model allows the most appropriate appraisal method to be selected for a given type of technology project, and from this provide the basis of a thorough appraisal. This helps to avoid the immediate rejection of projects which cannot be assessed on financial measures alone, or which have a combination of financial and non-financial benefits.

- They recommend that:

  1. Return on investment should be applied in traditional cost reduction projects, as the benefits are hard and very measurable

  2. Cost–benefit analysis should be applied in well-defined circumstances. Unlike return on investment, it has the capability to deal with a wide range of benefits that are both tangible and intangible in nature – as long as there is consensus on how the intangibles are to be measured. The method typically fails where this consensus cannot be achieved, or where the realization of the intangible benefits seems unlikely

  3. Multi-objective, multi-criteria methods should be used in more complex situations. These techniques recognize that there are other measures of value apart from money, that different stakeholders will have different views on the value of the proposed benefits, and that the majority of organizations find it easier to express their preferences in relative rather than absolute terms. As you would expect, such approaches require more effort to apply than the standard financial techniques, such as return on investment, but this effort is worth it because they are designed to cope with large and complex projects with major organizational impacts.

SMART PEOPLE TO HAVE ON YOUR SIDE

should consider staging the funds they give to their technology investments. What normally happens is that all the money is set aside and will be used until the project is either delivered or it comes back for more funding, which can often be a bad sign. A much better approach would be to provide the project with funding for each stage – initial investigation, design, build, test and implement. Each stage would seek funding and assess the risks and benefits associated with its completion. At the end of each stage the progress would be assessed and the next stage planned. In addition the benefits case would be revisited to assess whether they are still achievable. All this would be taken together and a decision made whether to continue with the project or not. If the investment is to progress, further funding will be made available.

Pulling the plug

What is it about technology that can cause smart people to make dumb decisions? I see companies investing a lot of money on IT initiatives that don't meet the minimum daily requirement for common sense. It's not that the ideas are bad – in fact, most of them aren't. But they are not well thought out.

Susan Cramm

One of the best things a venture capitalist will do is pull out of a bad investment. Staging the funding will reduce their losses and will allow them to invest in their next venture or transfer the money to a more successful one in their portfolio. As a result the venture capitalist does not become too wedded to a particular project and will analyse it in an objective way. Organizations should learn from this. Unfortunately they are notorious for not terminating problem projects and sparing themselves pain later on. Instead they typically carry on regardless and allow ego to get in the way of reality. There is no doubt that organizations must be more willing to accept the value that failure can bring. No matter how painful, it is better to learn from mistakes than pretend that they never happened only to repeat them at a later date. Equally, indiscriminately sacking members of a project team serves no other purpose other than to stifle innovation. A healthy attitude toward failure is required as it allows organizations to become more innovative, take calculated risks, and learn when things do not go as well as planned. To be successful at this requires a number of shifts in the way organizations behave when a project fails. These include:

- Committing to the termination of projects for the right reasons.

- Committing to learning from failures, as a means of improving project success.

- Committing to the appropriate management of project personnel once a project has failed.

- Committing to the sharing of knowledge of failures across the organization as a means of increasing sensitivity.

- Recognizing that failure will always be a potential outcome of any project and as a result maintain the vigilance required to prevent it from happening.

The purpose of staging the funding can help the termination of technology investments and as long as this is coupled with objectivity, organizations can prevent diasters in which their projects become money sinks. The warning signs that the smart organization needs to look out for are discussed in Chapter 6.

It is clear that managing the risks associated with the introduction of new technology is an essential competency and one that begins with the financial management of the investment. Lewis Branscomb and Philip

Auerswald, authors of *Taking Technical Risks*, offer the following strategies for dealing with the combination of technical (product) failure and market failure when introducing new technologies:

- *Obtain more cash at a given point in the future.* Organizations with successful technological innovations focus on both the manufacture of their own proprietary products and some liquidity event that ensures their investors see a return on their investment. This includes initial public offerings that raise additional capital through the stock market. The capital raised is then used to continue product and business development as well as providing the venture capitalist with a return on their investment. This was a typical approach adopted by the dotcoms

- *Obtain the same cash inflows but sooner.* This usually involves establishing partnership deals with third parties.

- *Reduce cash outflows.* Because technical innovations can become money sinks, organizations can adopt a number of strategies to reduce the risks they face. They can enter into partnership deals (as above). They can delay product launch until the product is robust enough to reduce the market's acceptance. Although there is always a risk attached to any delay, the consequences of releasing an unreliable product can be worse, especially if it is being launched globally (such as through the Internet). Other strategies include adopting a risk–reward approach with backers where the amount they receive as the return on their investment varies according to the level of risk they take. This is particularly useful if the backer is well known within the target market as they can serve to reduce the level of market risk.

- *Obtain the same outflows, but later.* Stage payments based upon technology performance allows the product and market risks to be managed more effectively. This is a common technique used by venture capitalists as a way of managing their financial risk, but is also a good method for managing the risks associated with product failure

- *Reduce the risks of cash inflows.* Any product worth its salt should be capable of bringing in more money than was invested in it. It is a sad fact that this is often not the case. Therefore organizations must take a long hard look at the market risks before product development starts, during its development and prior to its launch. This can be achieved through market research and working closely with the ultimate customers of the product

- *Trickle-up rather than trickle-down product development.* Many products are aimed at the high end of the market and tend to be very sophisticated, functionally rich and as a consequence prone to failure. Also, when a complex product is launched, organizations then have to battle with the problem of making a cheaper, less complex variant for other markets. This can be difficult. The alternative strategy is to begin with a simple product and build its level of sophistication over time. In this way it is possible to iron out the major manufacturing and product glitches early on. The Japanese used this approach very successfully with the development of charge-coupled devices, which are now integral to every laptop computer. They followed a performance enhancing process rather than a cost reducing one.

Of course, technology imposes risks across the complete lifecycle and it is essential that we manage them and manage them well (as we will see later).

Implications for technology management

So we can conclude that in many respects investing in a new technology project is no different from investing in a new business start-up. Both share common characteristics, including:

- They require large sums of money.

- They require careful management.

- They only have once chance of succeeding.

- They are often very risky and require effective risk management.

- They require careful financial management.

The smart organization knows that to manage their technology investment requires them to consider the costs very carefully. They also know that they have to be ruthless when it comes to cutting funding. This ensures they do not waste their financial resources and allows them to invest in other projects. But smart technology management is not just about acting like a venture capitalist, it also means recognizing that, when it comes to technology management, benefits should drive everything. This aspect of smart thinking is discussed in the next chapter.

3

Smart Thinking II – Benefits Drive Everything

W.H. Smith

W.H. Smith saved £150,000 by using business intelligence software to build customer retention rates. In the first year of use, W.H. Smith saw its productivity increase by 75 per cent with a further rise of 35 per cent in the second year.

(M. Holland, *Computing*, 16 Dec. 2001.)

SMART VOICES

Benefits, what benefits?

The rationale behind the computerization of the 1950s was to gain the increased productivity that had been established by the Industrial Revolution, when great tranches of manual labour were eradicated through the application of modern machinery. Therefore, it would be reasonable to assume that the growth of computerization and rising investment trends since the early automation projects of the 1950s and 1960s were the result of productivity payoffs from these investments. If coupled with the post-war boom, itself fuelled by computerization, it is easy to see why most organizations, especially those in the United States and Europe, were at that time unconcerned as to whether IT offered a good return on investment. It was not until the late 1970s, when the dominance of the United States and European economies began to wane, that organizations started to question the high levels of IT investment. But even then, the issue was clouded by Moore's Law. However, by the late 1980s, questions were being raised about the limited productivity payoffs from IT as assessments of the true economic impacts revealed a far from rosy picture:[1]

- Since the introduction of office-based computer systems in the 1960s, United States investment in IT has been in the region of $4 trillion. By making comparisons of average gross domestic product for the period 1973–1983 it becomes apparent that up to $30 billion per year has been lost in output as a result of the low productivity returns from information technology investments.

- While manufacturing productivity in the United States grew at 4.1 per cent per year during the 1980s, white collar productivity rose by just 0.28 per cent a year, despite the massive expenditure in office technology.

- Buying computers and related technology appears to be a little more

[1]For a detailed review of the payback from IT investments, see Landauer (1995)

than 13 per cent less productive than other forms of capital investments.

This analysis is born out of observation, where it seems that, rather than reduce the amount of office-based work, IT appears to increase it. For example, in 1968 United States hospitals employed around 440,000 administrators to serve approximately 2.4 million patients daily. By 1992, the number of administrative positions had increased to 2.2 million while the number of daily patients had dropped to approximately 840,000. During this time there had been massive investment in technology to improve the administration of patients.

The debate about the so-called productivity paradox has been raging for well over a decade and is still not resolved. For some, we have entered a new world, based on intangibles and knowledge, for others nothing has really changed. So, the first camp believe that the way we measure productivity needs to change to take into account the way knowledge is produced and applied; the second believe that technology investments (well, at least IT) do not improve productivity and in many cases actually reduce it (so aptly illustrated in the US hospital example). Much of this debate has stemmed from the growth in US productivity which

---

McKinsey

- Global strategy and management consultancy.
- Conducted an extensive study on return on investment from IT.
- Concluded that the US productivity miracle was down to a combination of factors, including innovation, economic factors such as the cost of borrowing, and the competitive environment.
- Found that the impact of investments in IT on productivity varied considerably across the economy.

SMART
PEOPLE
TO HAVE
ON YOUR
SIDE

between 1995 and 2000 was running at an annualized rate of 2.5 per cent, well above its 1972–1995 run rate of 1.4 per cent. Much of this increase was put down to investments in technology (principally IT) which had increased dramatically over the same period. The simplistic conclusion was that there was a direct link between the two. It appears that this is not the case (see Smart People to Have on Your Side: McKinsey), as there are plenty of reasons why achieving benefit returns from technology investments appear to be so elusive. Here are just a few:

- The large number of technology platforms, software systems, operating systems and packages available impacts productivity for two reasons. Firstly, because each has its own language, syntax and unique make-up, it can be difficult to move from one system to another without an associated dip in productivity during familiarization, or refamiliarization. Secondly, despite notable attempts by the IT industry to provide genuinely compatible technology platforms and systems, there still remain significant issues in getting different systems and hardware platforms to communicate. This means that there can be more breakpoints between systems, and hence a greater opportunity for the introduction of errors, especially where this involves the rekeying of data from one system to another.

- As software is updated, it typically involves an increase in the number of features it provides. Such functionality creep is standard practice in IT as the desire to increase the capabilities of the technology is highly seductive. For example, IBM will be releasing a long-overdue upgrade to their Lotus Notes product which is expected to add an additional 1,000 functions; who needs that many and, more importantly, who is going to use them? The trouble is most people want simplicity and will not use all of the additional functions, let alone those that may already exist. More on this in the next chapter.

- The unreliability of software is one of the greatest contributory factors to limited productivity growth. As software and systems have become more complex, it has become harder to test them thoroughly and as a result there is a greater opportunity for them to fail. Also, because of its complexity, software has a tendency to crash when least expected. What is more worrying is that, because of the underlying complexity, it can be difficult to replicate the exact conditions that caused the failure in the first place. It is well known that software downtime costs businesses very dear in lost productivity, running into billions per year.

- With so much software on the desktop the opportunity for employees to avoid productive work in favour of tinkering with their software packages is very seductive. Employees with access to the average desktop's software can send personal emails, write personal letters, and play with their electronic diaries, all of which serve to reduce productivity. Increasingly, with access to the Internet, or their company's Intranet, the opportunity to surf for information is appealing, but again serves to distract them from their day-to-day activity. For example, the average US employee is spending 90 minutes a day visiting websites unrelated to his or her job and Canadian employees are wasting 800 million hours a year doing the same (Robins, 2002).

Flipping the cost–benefit equation

Organizations get it fundamentally wrong when they appraise their technology investments. All too often they focus on the costs first and then attempt to identify benefits that can be claimed to justify the costs. A much better way to deal with this is to flip the equation so that it forces people to think about the benefits before they assess the costs. Therefore the next time you have a business problem, spend time con-

Susan Cramm

Susan Cramm of Value-dance provides this advice when thinking about your next technology investment:

1. Define the rules. This means making it clear that some kind of business benefit must be derived from the investment

2. Use operational measures. Although difficult to measure the benefits directly, it is an excellent idea to use existing operational measures such as product quality, customer service and cycle time because changes in these will have a financial impact. Understanding how the technology investment impacts these and other similar measures is a valuable way to assess and hence measure benefit

3. Be unreasonable. Unwrapping this means ensuring that the project is capable of stretching people through high expectations. People are more able to commit and deliver to stretching targets. Of course, this does not mean impossible targets because it is equally well known that no one buys into these

4. Stage the funding. As we saw in Chapter 2, this means acting like a venture capitalist. In this way it is possible to ensure focus on the benefits of the investment are always high on the agenda

5. Invest in the front line. This is where small changes can have big impacts. Effective technology investments must focus on those that deliver the service. Failing to do so can result in big impacts, but in this case negative ones

6. Evaluate the portfolio. A mixed portfolio of technology projects that addresses the need to innovate as much as maintain existing products and services is essential. So is an annual or bi-annual review that assesses progress and relates this to benefit.

sidering what benefits could be derived from solving the problem. And when doing this attempt to place a nominal value on them. Most things can be traced to one of three categories of benefit:

- Cost reduction

- Cost displacement (moving costs to another part of the business, where it could add more value)

- Revenue enhancement

As you place each of the benefits into one or more of the monetary categories above, think about what might change or how things will be done differently, as this will help to define the technology project later on. Once you have reviewed the benefits of solving the business problem, you can then discuss it with the senior executives of the company. The conversation might go a little bit like this:

CIO: "I've been toying with the problems we have been having with our suppliers recently and believe we ought to be able to solve it"

CEO: "And how much is this going to cost me?"

CIO: "Actually, I think it is a better idea to consider what the benefits might be if we solved the problem before we move onto costs."

CEO: "Go on."

CIO: "I've analysed the benefits and tracked these to targets for reducing and displacing costs as well as increasing revenue, and believe we could save between $600,000 to $900,000 annually."

CEO: "Looking at your figures, Peter, I think this may even be an underestimate of the savings, as I think there are some other categories you have missed."

CIO: "Okay, but even if we take the figures I have here, how much would you be willing to invest to secure these benefits?"

CEO: "I would be prepared to spend around $1.5 million."

CIO: "Excellent, I will use this as the provisional project budget and come back to you with how we will achieve these savings in a couple of weeks."

The conversation is of course fictitious, but the concept is very important. By forcing the CEO to focus on the benefits first, the CIO shifted the attention from the cost side of the technology investment to the benefits side. In doing so he has:

- Created a much better understanding of what the project budget will be by asking how much the CEO would be willing to invest in order to secure the benefits.

- Clarified the likely benefits that could be secured from solving the problem and ensured the CEO gave additional input before any work has gone into considering how the project might be structured or what it might deliver.

- Begun to raise the importance of benefits before the project has even started. In essence he has started to create the reception strategy (see Chapter 7).

The real benefit associated with flipping the relationship between costs and benefits is around establishing realism. Most organizations think

Marilyn Parker and Robert Benson

- Authors of *Information Economics*.
- Believe that traditional forms of project appraisal do not suit technology projects.
- Developed the concept of Information Economics, which allows organizations to make a more comprehensive assessment of the benefits they should expect from their technology investments
- State that it is possible to asses value by reviewing the investment across two domains:

  1. The business domain, which covers the benefit side of the investment:
     - return on investment
     - strategic match
     - competitive advantage
     - management information support
     - legislative implementation
     - organizational risk

  2. The technology domain, which addresses the risks associated with the investment:
     - strategic architecture alignment
     - definitional uncertainty risk
     - technical uncertainty risk
     - information system infrastructure risk

about the benefits of their technology investments as an afterthought and do not have the quality of thinking required to ensure they are realistic or achievable. As a result everyone forgets about the benefits and moves onto their next issue. The other value that this approach provides is a clearer picture of project budget. Once again, organizations can be accused of woolly thinking. When a technology project is costed out, senior executives often seek reductions in the budget because they cannot see the benefits to justify the spend (because no one has really thought out what the benefits might be). Unfortunately this makes the project all the more difficult to achieve, leads to project heroics (see Chapter 6) and ends up costing more than expected, and in some cases might even fail. Smart organization's are those that think benefits first and costs second.

Tesco

Tesco, the UK's largest retailer and grocer, has gone from strength to strength with its online ordering system. The £40 million investment, which started small in 1995, has evolved from one that depended on faxes being sent to stores once the online order was received, to one that is linked to stores' computers and trolleys with onboard computers. It has over one million registered customers and processes 70,000 orders a week. The system has recently been adopted by the US company Safeway and is a role model of Internet grocery shopping. Its success is down to learning from earlier failures, focusing on in-store pickers rather than relying on warehouse facilities, and its simplicity.

(S. Voyle, *Financial Times*, 30 Jun./1 Jul. 2001)

Tough questions to ask before you invest

Equally important as understanding the benefits of investing in technology is assessing the risks that it might pose to the organization. Organizations often focus on the upside of the investment without attending to the potential for disaster. Here are seven questions that every organization should ask themselves before they invest in their next technology project:

1. How dependent will you be on the new system, and what are the implications of failure?

On July 22 1962, a program with a tiny omission in an equation cost US taxpayers $18.5 million when an Atlas-Agena rocket was destroyed in error. In 1983, when the Aegis Navy battle management system underwent its first operational testing, it was only capable of shooting down six out of seventeen targets when presented three at a time. It was designed to shoot down twenty targets but failed because of a software error. This system was latterly linked to the shooting down of the Iranian Airbus 320 by the *USS Vincennes* in 1988; the software incorrectly identified the Airbus as an F-14 military jet. Tiny errors can have significant impacts, especially when the software controls an organizational, or in the case of the *USS Vincennes*, military, function. This is a particular problem with very complex software systems, and something that can seemingly never be resolved. Therefore, when considering the next technology investment, organizations should ask themselves how dependent will they be on it once it is in use. If its failure at a future date presents no significant operational problems, the level of business continuity can be minimal. However, where the system is essential to the operation of the business – because it might be safety critical, provide enterprise-wide data, or be operationally vital – the level of business continuity planning must, as a consequence be much higher.

2. How much testing is needed?

Knowing the answer to question 1, how much time should be given to testing? Clearly, if an organization can assess how dependent it might be on a new technology, it ought to be able to estimate the level of testing that should be undertaken to ensure it is as reliable as it needs to be. This is perhaps an impossible question to answer for many reasons, and not least because of the invisible and complex nature of software. For example, the software that operates the Space Shuttle runs to 25,600,000 lines, which makes it impossible to test. And, because of the nature of the Shuttle, it is controlled by five separate systems, even though it only needs one to operate it. The four additional systems provide the necessary level of redundancy to ensure that if one system fails another can take over – clearly a good example of tailoring business continuity to the level of software dependency. It is, of course, well known that even thorough testing of a relatively small system can take literally thousands of years if every possible path through the software is tested. As a result, organizations have adopted various approaches to test software as much as they can, while still delivering it within a reasonable time frame. For example, the use of redundancy which relies on the probability of two identical components failing being less than the probability of one component failing can ensure systems are less likely to fail. Thus the Space Shuttle, which has four redundant systems, has a low probability of failure.

Another technique, known as diversity, is particularly important for safety critical systems. Here, the same system functionality is built using different hardware and software. Therefore if the primary system fails, it is unlikely that the back-up system would fail in the same way because it would not contain the same systematic faults. Again, in order to safeguard the Space Shuttle and its crew, its controlling software includes this additional safety net. Care in testing is vital, and it is important to recognize that even small changes can have major consequences, as DSC communications found in June and early July 1991, when the standard fourteen-week testing cycle was omitted after a software change. The resultant outages affected telephone users along the Eastern Seaboard of the United States.

3. What are the external implications of software error?

With an increasingly wired world, in which business is conducted electronically, the implications of software failure, or the transfer of poor information can be significant. We have to consider the effects of failure much more widely than before because the reach of technology is so much greater.

4. It is tempting to solve every problem with technology

Unfortunately some problems cannot be solved that way. It is also tempting to follow the advice of the technology salesmen who are employed to make IT appear so powerful and effective. Equally, the allure of following the competition and mirroring their IT investments can be compelling. Believing that technology is the only arbiter of success can be a mistake as some systems don't achieve anything. Therefore, when considering their next technology project, senior managers ought to request additional information about why the system is the right one for the business. Answers such as, "the competition have just implemented something similar", "the computer press are raving about it", or "it will solve all our data problems once and for all" are insufficient, and arguably indefensible blanket statements with little substance. It is important to know what alternatives have been considered, and why they have been rejected. If, for example, the system does not fit with the organization's strategic direction, or does not provide a good operational fit (that is, the ability to add significant operational value), this should raise some questions about its viability. This presupposes, of course, that the organization has a strategic direction in the first place; many do not.

The two dimensions of operational and strategic fit are quite important, as they provide the balance between the here and now requirements of the organization, and the future direction of the business. Naturally, in cases where the intention is to change the working practices of the organization, the operational fit should be assessed against the new operating model, not the existing one. Where the coupling between these two dimensions is either strong or weak, the decision to adopt, or reject the new investment should be quite straightforward. Where, however, they are not, this can be used to force the organization to question the value in a bit more detail, and demand more in the way of justification. Hence, where the strategic and operational fit are out of alignment, it is not a case of rejection, but one of further investigation which should either lead to the project's rejection or adoption. The ultimate goal should be to establish a positive (that is, adopt or reject) outcome, as opposed to a "let's suck it and see" approach to accepting the project.

5. What are the implications on the existing technical and organizational infrastructures?

IT systems are rarely isolated, and, as a consequence, they are likely to impact more than just the business environment – the systems environment is increasingly an important factor to consider. When a new technology is introduced, it is likely that it will alter the existing mode of operations – new relationships have to be built, new interfaces created, new processes and information flows developed. It is necessary, therefore, to take an holistic approach to understanding the impact a new information system is likely to have on the business. This requires a deeper analysis of the role the technology is expected to play, but also an understanding of what other systems have to be altered, and what constraints these existing systems may impose on the new technology being introduced. All of this can add value, and hence provide balance to any business case because it allows some of the additional project work, and associated costs, to be flushed out. It will also provide a better indication of the investment required to achieve the anticipated returns.

6. Have the human consequences of the system been fully considered?

It seems trite to say, but people are an important part of any technology. The technical determinism of IT often seeks to minimize both their input during the project, and their involvement with the system once implemented. Any technology project should be about the optimization of technology and the human capital of the organization. Why? People have strengths and weaknesses, but their greatest asset is that they are motivated by outcomes, are especially good at recognizing patterns, and are able to take into account factors which are external to the system. Computers, on the other hand, are bad at these things, and dispassionate about outcomes. Although it is obvious to suggest that the relative strengths of the two should be optimized, for the last forty years there has been limited success in this respect – technology has always won. Even within sophisticated computer systems, the most fault-tolerant and robust element is the operator. However, reducing their input to trouble shooting when the system malfunctions is not a good use of their skills, particularly when these systems are safety critical. This can pose significant risks, especially when we consider how little people know about the inner workings of the system, or the business processes it is designed to support. As more of an organization's business processes are subsumed within these black boxes, this lack of understanding will increase, and make it difficult for companies to adjust and add to their systems without making them unstable. Indeed, I have come across situations where business-critical systems have not been enhanced because people do not know how they work – there is a very real risk of system failure if they change it. One must always remember that technology is designed by fallible human beings. Eliminating human contact within the key business processes of an organization can be highly dangerous, especially when technology breaks down. It is not, therefore, unreasonable to consider the impacts on the staff at the time of the business case. Naturally, the introduction of a new information system may lead to a reduction in headcount, but for those who remain, it would be worth considering how their roles in the organization will be affected. This is, of course, not just about training, but job content and satisfaction. But, it has to be said, this is rarely considered as organizations attempt to complete their technology projects on time. Indeed those who believe the computerization of the workplace is creating an electronic sweatshop, are not far from the truth. For example, people who work in call centres have to endure conditions that lead to musculoskeletal disorders, migraines and eye strain. In addition they are monitored electronically, and, in extreme cases, have to ask to go to the lavatory. It should come as no surprise that call centres suffer from high absenteeism and staff turnover. It is clear that within technology projects you ignore people at your peril

7. Can you afford the project to be late, or fail, and what are the implications?

A question that is rarely asked, but I believe is very necessary. Asking this question before the project commences can be very enlightening. Clearly if this project is strategically important, the organization would not wish it to fail, and may not tolerate it being late. For example Enterprise Resource Planning systems (such as SAP, BAAN and PeopleSoft) are currently seen as being pivotal to running today's complex businesses. The projects that implement these systems are major undertakings and are often seen as being strategically important, and yet, according to new research, are usually late, over budget, fail to meet business expectations, and miss their return on investment targets. Equally, the gold rush into e-commerce was wholly dependent upon the success of the technology once implemented, and for many organizations this proved to be fools' gold. The thing is, when a project is running late, it is ultimately impacting its return on investment. If the project is significantly over budget and late, its viability must come into question, because with it costing significantly more, and taking longer to implement, the ability to achieve the benefits will be dramatically reduced. Therefore, as organizations develop their next business case, five scenarios should be added to force an assessment of the implications of the project running late, being over budget or failing. These five scenarios are:

- The project runs to time and budget, and delivers all that is expected of it.

- The project is late and/or over budget but delivers all of the expected functionality.

- The project runs to time and budget, but is descoped to meet these constraints.

- The project is late and/or over budget but delivers a reduced functionality.

- The project fails, and is terminated before, or shortly after implementation.

Pagoda

- A specialist consultancy focusing on delivering complex change.

- Conducted an extensive survey into IT projects and concluded successful projects, and hence IT investments, can only provide real benefit returns if they deal with the change (people, process and organization) elements effectively.

- Suggest ten ground rules for gaining full benefit from IT investments:

  1. Develop a culture that welcomes change.

  2. Ensure operational managers take responsibility for initiating change and getting the most out of it.

  3. Treat IT as one part of an integrated change project.

  4. Ensure senior managers set clear and mutually compatible objectives for the investment's benefits.

  5. Avoid narrow technical and financial objectives which inhibit broader change.

  6. Never omit the human and organizational activities at the planning stage.

  7. Ensure that the way change is introduced reflects the future business environment (in essence how things will look once the project is complete).

  8. Ensure project managers involve staff in the design and implementation of the change.

  9. Incorporate learning opportunities within the project.

  10. Create excellent two-way communication with those affected by the change, using their feedback to modify the approach if necessary.

These scenarios ensure that whoever is charged with overseeing the investment are focused on the outcome and benefits. This also makes it easier to kill the project if it turns out to be a lemon.

Think cost, benefit and risk

Organizations like to think about their projects in terms of time, cost and quality. The idea behind this is that if a project is well managed it will come in on time, within budget and deliver the required functionality to the expected level of quality; in essence, delivering a product that can be considered to be fit for purpose. I believe that this fails to address two critical elements: benefit and risk. Projects are risky undertakings that are expected to deliver some kind of benefit to the organization. And although both time and quality are essential elements to technology projects, both relate to risk and benefit. For example, if a technology project takes longer than planned it will impact on how soon and possibly how much benefit will be realized. And very often it affects the quality because the project might be descoped to bring it in. It is far better to view the project across the three dimensions of cost, benefit and risk because an effective technology project has to balance each of these in order to optimize the benefits. Understanding the impacts of risk on the likelihood of realizing the benefits allows the smart organization to pull the plug on those technology investments that are destined to failure. Equally, as the costs of a technology project increase, the benefits may decrease. Such information feeds into a technique known as cost–benefit–risk analysis or COBRA.

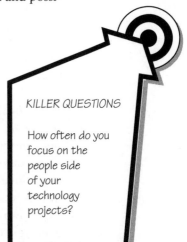

KILLER QUESTIONS

How often do you focus on the people side of your technology projects?

Finally, when the technology project is underway, don't forget to keep on monitoring the likelihood of these three elements.

Alan Fowler

- Founder of Isochron, a UK company specializing in benefits realization.
- Project acceleration and benefits realization expert.
- Believes that benefits can be achieved from technology projects if the following seven key points are met:

  1. Project outcomes are expressed in tangible terms.
  2. The impact of the project outcomes is tested against a balanced scorecard of all business value, revenue and cost drivers.
  3. Qualitative benefits must be estimated in cash terms.
  4. Benefits and costs are estimated with equal thoroughness.
  5. Project selection is based upon a balanced and rigorous assessment of return on investment.
  6. Benefits are directly linked to project milestones.
  7. Audits should be used to cancel any project that is misdirected and failing to provide benefit.

In the final analysis, technology investments do not create benefits on their own. Benefits only come with concerted action at the time of planning, during execution and once the project has been completed. Smart organizations recognize that a lot of effort is required and they are willing to invest in the time required to get it right. However, an important insight into getting better returns from your technology investments is to get away from thinking about technology. If you view them as products, you might get more benefits than you had ever expected. This product mindset is the subject of the next chapter.

4

Smart Thinking III – Think Product not Technology

Business people are totally dependent on technologists for their ability to create things that work. And technologists are totally dependent on business people to provide them with the tool for their efforts. This makes for an uneasy symbiosis.

Alan Cooper

SMART QUOTES

We know that it is impossible to engineer software in the same way that we can engineer a bridge. We also know that we never quite know how a technology product will behave until it is delivered. Both create problems for those who are tasked with developing software systems

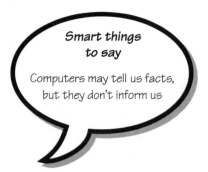

Smart things to say

Computers may tell us facts, but they don't inform us

whether they are for the internal market or the external one. The only difference, however, is that internal technology products have to be used; external ones can be left on the shelf.

The history of technology products, especially software, is not good. This is because they are developed with the wrong audience in mind and as a result come to market at the wrong time with too many flaws and errors. If we look at some of the major software-driven innovations of the last few decades we can see that many were not mature enough for their markets, either in terms of their reliability or their audience. The early fly-by-wire aircraft that literally fell out of the sky, the websites that failed because they had too many bugs and no business model to ever make them viable, the WAP phones that no one wanted, the IT systems that failed to work, and so on. Without some smart thinking, we are destined to continue to make the same errors time and time again. And this smart thinking resides in the ability to think in terms of end-products, not technology.

Once you can make this distinction you can then begin to develop technology products that will serve the customer (inside or outside of the

SMART
ANSWERS
TO TOUGH
QUESTIONS

Q. Why should we worry, after all every software system has bugs in them and these should be accepted as part of the process

A. We should be concerned because bugs cost money. According to the United States Defense Department and the Software Engineering Institute at Carnegie Mellon University, there are typically between 5 and 15 flaws in every 1,000 lines of code and tracking down each bug can take 75 minutes and fixing them takes 2–9 hours each. On the outside, that's 150 hours, or roughly $30,000, to ensure every 1,000 lines of code is error free.

organization) more effectively. And, as a result make the management of technology that bit simpler. This avoids some of the common problems associated with technology products, including:

KILLER QUESTIONS

How much money do you want to waste on technology?

- Vapourware – software that does not really exist, because it is never delivered.

- Shelfware – software that is developed, delivered, but never used.

- Bloatware – software that is so function rich that we could never hope to use all of it, or indeed a mere 10 per cent.

What we know from great product innovators

Whatever your view of technology, the one thing is clear is that it must be viewed as a product. This necessitates a shift in thinking from one in which technology and all it entails is the dominant factor to one in which the ultimate utility and value to the end-user or customer is the overriding factor. The great product innovators know this and it useful for those involved with managing technology to appreciate how they

What wakes customers up . . . is product leadership, a company displaying the ability and determination to make products that customers recognize as superior – products that deliver real benefit and performance improvements. This is a hard lesson to learn, and many companies learn it only after suffering through customer indifference to their boring products.

Michael Treacy and Fred Wiersema

SMART QUOTES

achieve their product excellence. Products are the key to corporate prosperity because no matter if they are sold externally or used internally they have the ability to generate revenue and value. Clearly if a product is sold externally and the market loves it, it will sell in large numbers and create huge revenues. Internal products are equally important because they support an organization and its activities. If these do not work, or they slow the organization down, revenues can be lost, costs can increase and the ability to be operationally efficient can be severely impacted. Thus thinking in product terms is important.

Thinking in this way requires those charged with managing technology, which includes its development to:

- Understand why products fail.

- Recognize the factors that make product development successful.

- Select a process that can be used for developing and launching internal technology products as effectively as those sold externally.

SMART QUOTES

For years, entrepreneurs – from aspiring dotcom millionaires to downshifters opening tea shops – have been rushing into new ventures without really understanding the market or the consumer. Yet this cause of failure is well known and has been for 20 years.

Carl Franklin

Products fail for one of four reasons (see Cooper, 2001):

1. *Poor market research.* Products often fail because the real needs of the customer have not been fully identified or understood.

2. *Technical problems.* The product can sometimes end up being

scrapped because, from a technical standpoint, it turns out to be impossible to build.

3. *Insufficient marketing effort.* It is wrongly assumed that the product will sell itself, so it is unnecessary to spend any time convincing the buyer that it is something they want.

4. *Bad timing.* Sometimes products fail because they miss the window of opportunity, times move on and the customers do not want it. The opposite is also true, as there are occasions when a product will fail because it is launched before it is really needed.

If we look at technology products, and especially those that are created in-house, such as information systems, we can see that the pitfalls identified above are very applicable. If you think of an new IT system, how many times have the requirements been poorly identified? Market research in this sense involves gaining a detailed understanding of the business and end-user needs of the new system. But, this is an often poorly executed phase of the project. Technical problems too dog most technology projects because the technologists do not understand the real requirements. They also fail to understand that people require simplicity and reliability not complexity. Technical problems are often at the root cause of most IT fiascos, such as the UK's National Air Traffic Control Centre at Swanick, the London Ambulance System, the US CONFIRM travel reservation system, and so on. Technology projects also suffer from a lack of marketing. No one explains to the end-user community what the technology will mean to them and the way they work. As a result there tends to be more resistance to change than necessary, the IT system may be rejected and the benefits do not materialize. And finally, there is bad timing. If the technology project is over-engineered and as a result takes longer than anticipated to complete, the business may have moved on and the product may no longer be required. All too often, no one tells the project team and they only find out when the project is finished.

SMART
PEOPLE
TO HAVE
ON YOUR
SIDE

Thomas Edison

- Nineteenth-century inventor.
- Invented over 1,300 products and had over 1,000 patents to his name.
- Understood what it meant to produce useful and reliable products.
- Father of the modern-day product development process.

So what else can we learn from the great product innovators? According to Robert Cooper, author of *Winning at New Products*, identifying what makes a new product successful is a lot harder than understanding why it fails. He cites the following factors, based on a number of studies by various consultancies and academics:

- The product needs to offer the customer unique benefits and value for money.
- There needs to be a strong market orientation.
- The ability to leverage internal technologies.
- The market launch is well executed.
- The research and development process is well executed.
- The product is high margin.
- The end-to-end processes from creating the product through to selling it are well managed and coordinated.

- There must be a good fit between the technology and marketing functions.

- Top management support is present throughout.

- The management style is one that facilitates innovation.

- Feedback and learning from previous product launches is embedded into the processes.

- There is strong strategic alignment.

- There is effective risk management.

Taking these studies into account, Cooper derived fifteen critical success factors for product development:

1. The organization must develop a unique and superior product.

2. The organization and product development process must be both market driven and customer focused.

3. The product has an international orientation.

4. The impact of the product is fully understood before it is developed – what Cooper terms as doing your homework.

5. Products, and the projects designed to deliver them are well defined.

6. The product launch is well executed with solid marketing.

7. The right organizational environment exists, including its structure and culture.

8. Top management support the complete process.

9. The core competencies of the company must be leveraged.

10. The product must be attractive.

11. Products that will not add value are killed off during the development process.

12. The product development process is well defined, consistently applied and repeatable.

13. The right skilled resources are available.

14. Speed and quality are managed in concert (one is not compromised for the other).

15. The product development process is staged to allow go/no-go decisions to be made more easily.

Although clearly directed at the creation of products that will be ultimately sold on the open market, the majority of these factors are just applicable to the internal technology product. It is also clear that many of these are ignored, or probably not even thought of in the first place in the traditional technology project. All too often, the project team focuses on the technology at the expense of making it fit for purpose and meet the needs of the internal customers. Taking a product view should begin to force those involved with technology investments to take a closer look at marketing their products more carefully and avoid the pitfalls of thinking technology first, and product second.

SMART VOICES

The Palm Pilot

The Palm Pilot is the market leading product in the personal digital assistant (PDA) market. Why? Because it has been produced as a product first and a technology second. It has successfully integrated technology with everyday need. Its design is based upon three principles: simplicity, wearability and connectivity.

The adoption lifecycle – why it matters

Thinking about products is a great start, but has to be augmented with an understanding of who the product is intended for. This is where the adoption cycle can help. Very simply, the adoption lifecycle allows us to understand what people look for in a new technology product. The lifecycle consists of five stages – innovators, early adopters, early majority, late majority and late adopters (Figure 4.1).

* *Innovators* are those people who love technology for technology's sake. They will seek out the latest technological innovation because they are fascinated by it and technology's advance in general. The fact that the product might not fulfil any meaningful purpose or have any real utility does not deter them. When it comes to software they pride themselves in finding the bugs and design flaws and are not that concerned with the errors themselves, but more in finding them. Indeed, these are people who are willing to accept a flawed product for the

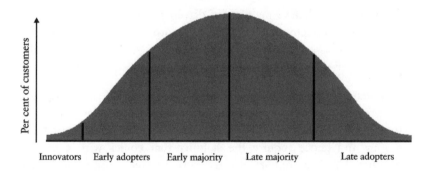

Figure 4.1 The product lifecycle.

... take the products considered to be great technological successes of the 20th century: the telephone, photocopier, fax, video recorder, PC, internet, mobile phone. Now think of the technology that frustrates you: it's probably the same list, since most of them are difficult to use. They work. But they fail you. It's not that these products don't function. Businesses put technical products through rigorous test procedures and user-acceptance testing cycles before they are released. Indeed, there's a whole industry sector that specializes in technology testing. But what they are evaluating is whether the product works. What they should be testing is *how* it works.

Lucy Kimbell

sake of innovation. Unsurprisingly, innovators are a small percentage of a product's audience.

- *Early adopters.* These are the non-technologists amongst us who will buy a product early because they are able to look beyond the technology and see some utility and benefit to it. This population is still quite small.

- *Early majority.* These people are driven by the need for practical applications of technology and are willing to wait until there is sufficient enthusiasm and take-up before they buy it. They are generally comfortable with new technology.

- *Late majority.* These are people who require a stable, well-functioning product that is either the industry standard or sufficiently popular to persuade them to buy. They are not entirely comfortable with technology and hence require the stability that comes with a mature product. They also require effective support mechanisms which they can draw upon when they run into difficulties.

- *Late adopters or laggards.* These are people who are unlikely to ever use the product out of choice. They may have to use it because it is embedded within another product, but in general they will never actively seek it out.

3G technology falls into the sloppy 'product looking for a solution' mode of thinking which leads to sensible organizations pouring vast sums of money into something that may not be much of a success. The model of Figure 4.1 assumes that the take up of any technology is a smooth transition from the innovators through to the late adopters. But, as Geoffrey Moore, author of *Crossing the Chasm* points out, it has one fundamental flaw – it fails to recognize that each category of buyer has different needs and that developing products that fulfil one category, say the early adopters, does not

> **Smart things to say**
>
> New technology attracts optimists and marginalizes luddites

---

3G technology

The 3G mobile telephony technology that was heralded as the next big mobile communications innovation looks as though it will fail to impress. This is a classic problem of developing a technology product without thinking about who actually wants or needs it. Recent examples of why it is being undermined include:

- Hutchison 3G admitting that its first customers will suffer months of dropped calls because of technical limitations of the new generation mobile phones.

- Telefonica of Spain and Sonera of Finland have abandoned their attempt to establish a new mobile business in Germany.

- Advances in existing 2G technology to allow video clips to be carried over mobile networks is undermining one of the biggest benefits of moving to 3G technology.

(P. Durham, *Sunday Times*, 28 Jul. 2001)

SMART VOICES

mean that it will be accepted by the next, which in this case would be the late majority. We can see from experience and from the history of IT that the majority of software and technology products released tend to be more suited to the innovators rather than the late majority, which is where the real benefits and revenues come from. The same often applies to those technologies developed and used internally. The problem is that such an approach results in poor benefit returns and ties organizations up in knots. When we couple acting like a venture capitalist with thinking products, we can start to see a powerful way of managing technology. The real benefit that the adoption cycle gives us is the ability to think very carefully about who will ultimately use the end product, as by understanding the nature of the end-user, or customer, it ought to be possible to develop a product that is going to be acceptable both in terms of its general utility and its reliability.

Smart product development processes

Although the next chapter discusses how technology projects should be managed, it is worth reviewing the process used by companies who are famous for launching products that we as consumers find useful. The typical product development process consists of five stages each separated by what product innovators term gates. These gates are essentially go/no-go decision points along the way and these typically link directly into the project's funding. The five stages are:

1. *Initial investigation*. Following an idea, the concept is explored in outline to determine if the technology is something the organization wishes to invest in and exploit

2. *Detailed investigation*. Assuming that this is something the organization is willing to commit to, some funding is provided to conduct a detailed investigation of the technology. This is likely to come up with options which themselves are fully costed and which provide an indication of the benefits that are likely to be generated and the resources required to develop and launch the product

3. *Development*. Once the idea has been assessed and is believed to add benefit to the organization (or external market), additional funds are released to develop the product. This requires the application of the requisite project and technology management expertise to make it successful. More on this in the next chapter

4. *Testing and validation*. Once the development has been completed, the product enters the crucial stage of testing and validation. Here it is tested against its market criteria, which would have been established during the detailed investigation stage. This will include market potential, reliability and so on. When launching an internal technology product, such as an IT system, it is necessary to not only system test it, but also test it with the business (known as business acceptance testing) to ensure it is ready to be launched.

5. *Launch*. Once fully tested the product can be launched.

Looking at the wider process through which technology is introduced within organizations, it is clear that most follow a similar, if not always well applied, process as the one above. The initial investigations are conducted under the guise of business systems options, development is normally extended to include such things as requirements analysis, design and build activities, testing is also extended to include unit test (components of the system), system test (the whole system), business acceptance testing (where the business test the final product), and launch is classified as implementation. So every technology project has a process. The problem is that the process is not always applied correctly or with much intelligence. This results in a much higher proportion of failures than we ought to expect and leads to problems with its usage.

When it comes to developing technology products like software systems there is an important distinction to make between the project lifecycle (initiate, plan, execute and terminate) and the product development lifecycle (analyse, design, build, test and implement). As the terms suggest, the former addresses the wider process of managing and co-ordinating the initiative as a whole, while the latter addresses the design and build activities of the product itself. There are essentially four product development lifecycle models that can be applied to technology projects:

1. Waterfall

This is probably the most commonly applied. In essence, the product development process follows one step after another sequentially with little or no feedback (Figure 4.2). This product development lifecycle is generally suited to stable environments where the requirements of the final product are well known and are unlikely to change. The history of the technology industry and internal IT system development suggests that this model is increasingly less applicable because it is poor at handling change and is not fast enough to cope with decreasing cycle times and demanding markets.

2. Evolutionary

Here a product is developed, but not the final one. The purpose of this

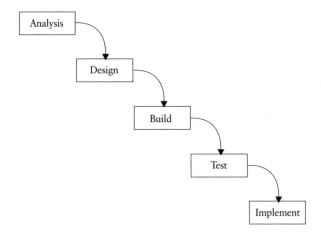

Figure 4.2 The waterfall product development lifecycle.

first product is to test it with the end-user (or customer) to assess whether it is fit for purpose. The approximate end product is understood, but is not known to a sufficient degree of detail to complete the development process, hence the need to adopt the evolutionary approach. Depending on the level of changes required, the feedback will lead to adjustments in analysis, design and build. Usually however, the majority of changes occur in the design and build stages of the process (Figure 4.3).

3. Staged or incremental build.

Here the final product is created in stages, with every build adding to the last. Usually the most important product features are developed first and the least important last. The design stage is broken into overall design, which will provide the blueprint of the final product. This is

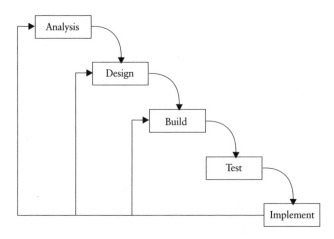

Figure 4.3 The evolutionary product development lifecycle.

then augmented and built as a series of increments. Each increment will include the standard steps of detailed design, build, test and implementation. After the desired number of increments the product is complete (Figure 4.4).

4. Prototyping

The fundamental purpose behind prototyping is to gain a clearer insight into what end product is actually required. This approach involves a significant amount of interaction with the end-user to establish their needs. The use of time boxing techniques can help to prevent too much time being spent on design without delivering a working prototype. A number of prototypes will be developed during the course of the project. Once the final prototype has been agreed, the project will pass

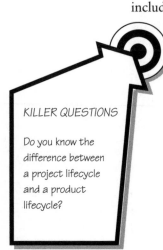

KILLER QUESTIONS

Do you know the difference between a project lifecycle and a product lifecycle?

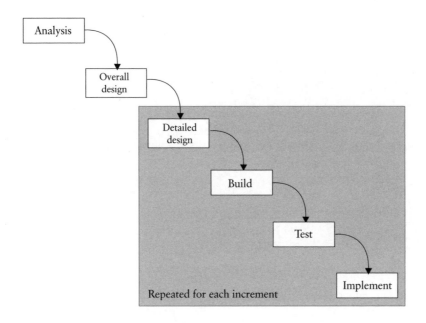

Figure 4.4 The staged or incremental product development lifecycle.

The product manager told me he wanted to build a product right for a change. He wanted to pay attention to quality, prevent feature creep, control the schedule, and have a predictable ship date. When the time came to actually to do the project, it became clear that getting the product to market quickly was the only real priority. Usability? *We don't have time.* Performance? *It can wait.* Maintainability? *Next project.* Testing? *Our users want the product now. Just get it out the door.*

Steve McConnell

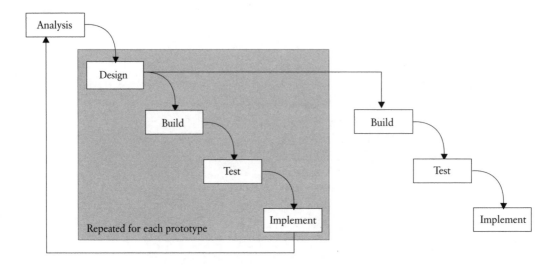

Figure 4.5 The prototyping product development lifecycle.

through the formal build, test and implement stages of the product development lifecycle (Figure 4.5).

It is often seductive to allow the last prototype to become the final product, but this can be very risky, especially if the process used to develop it is not as rigours as normal. It is important to remember that prototypes are usually unstable and contain numerous errors which is why it is critical to follow the last prototype with a more rigorous process to ensure the final product is of the appropriate quality.

The choice of product development lifecycle model depends on what is being built, and should take into account such things as the technology risks, how well the requirements for the end product are understood, how much change is expected during the process and how long is available to develop the product.

Wal-Mart

Wal-Mart have transformed the way they manage their stock using sophisticated IT systems and networks. By capturing detailed point of sale information at each of their stores, combining it and sending this back to suppliers,
Wal-Mart have increased the efficiency in inventory management, ordering and
shipping. Suppliers no longer have to send reps, instead receiving information
direct from Wal-Mart about what products are needed and where on a daily
basis.

Think personas not end-users[1]

Having a good product development lifecycle and understanding where
along the adoption cycle the end-user or customer sits is still not enough
to create a technology product that is world-class. The final part of the
equation rests with thinking in terms of personas.

One of the many issues that technology management presents to organizations is the attitude of the technologists to those who will use their
technology. Customer relationship management may be a critical to
business these days, but it seems to have passed the technologist by. This
may seem trivial but because the technologists fail to understand the
dynamics and real needs of those who will use their products, too many
of them end up as vapourware, shelfware, bloatware, or just plain difficult to use. This problem is not technological *per se*, but is associated
with the way people and technology interact. This has long been termed
the culture gap and it manifests itself in different ways, including:

---

[1]For a detailed discussion of personas, gaols and scenarios see, Cooper (1999).

- The non-specialist who either has a deep-seated mistrust of computers, or believes that anything is possible at the press of a button.

- The quasi-specialist, typically adept at developing end-user applications, such as spreadsheets, and databases, and who, by virtue of their own limited experiences in IT, believe the creation of information systems is a straightforward task.

- Senior management, who are increasingly finding it difficult to justify the escalating costs of computerization, particularly when it is so hard to see any significant return on investment. They are tiring of the hype and many believe IT has been oversold.

- Directors who do not, or will not, understand IT, believing it is someone else's problem. As a result they fail to keep up with the trends in technology and therefore fail to recognize the significance it may have on their organization.

SMART QUOTES

An IT system starts out for its users as an entity, created, in its details by an alien people – techies – and posing the problem of whether it really will be workable, cost effective, adequate, secure, upgradeable, compatible, etc. Techies are always moving the technology goal posts, increased penetration of IT continually increases an organization's exposure to risks of disruption. Thus for users, an IT system is always a problem.

Hales

But the real problem is not so much the inability to communicate or even the mistrust people have in new technology (itself based upon the poor experience they have had in the past) but more to do with the technologists not understanding who they are developing the product for. Very often, they spend too much time over-engineering the solution and adding lots of unnecessary features than thinking about who will be expected to use the product once it has been implemented. According to Alan Cooper, author of *The Inmates are Running the Asylum*, the answer to the problem lies in taking the trouble to understand the end-user and design the product for them. In other words, think of them as real people rather than abstractly as users. The term user is unhelpful because it is too general and can be interpreted in any way the developers like. Moving away from the user mindset means going beyond the usual process of asking them what they want and developing personas of the type of people who will be using the product once it is complete. This is a three step process:

KILLER QUESTIONS

Will you develop technologies that people want to use?

1. Generate personas

A persona is essentially a description of a hypothetical person that will be using the technology once it has been developed. Like any real person, they have a name, an age, a role in a company and a daily job to fulfil. The more specific these personas are, the more effective the product's design will be. The use of personas helps to remove the typical problem of believing the end-users are either dummies or experts and not creating anything in between for those people with intermediate knowledge and capabilities. One of the beauties of personas is that they help to eliminate the problem of the technologists developing features which they think are useful, but no one else does. It forces them to test every new feature against each persona and if is not relevant it is dropped from the product. Every project will have between three and twelve personas and within this population there will be a small number of primary personas who will be the main focus of the design and who must be satisfied with the final product.

2. Construct goals associated with personas

There are three types of goals that need to be considered: corporate goals, personal goals and practical goals. It is the practical goals that link the personal and corporate goals and focus more on the day-to-day aspects of a particular job. The use of these forces the developer to think beyond just the goals of the software, which is one reason why software is often poorly received by the users

3. Create scenarios

This describes how the personas will be using the technology. Three scenarios are usually required. The first is the daily use scenario which is what the end-user will do on a daily basis. This must be supported by the technology, although over time it is likely to evolve as their job evolves, or their expertise increases. This is the most important scenario as if it is not satisfied it is highly likely that the technology will be rejected. The second is the necessary use scenario. These are things that have to be performed but on an intermittent or occasional basis. The technology must support these, but does not require the flexibility associated with the daily use scenario. The third is the edge scenario these

Q. Why are IT professionals like drug pushers?

A. Because they both sell their products to users

are the rare events that require support. Unlike the other two, these scenarios are less important and do not require the rigour of design expected of the others. Users will be much more forgiving if these do not work than if the daily or necessary use scenarios fail. In most cases they should be de-emphasized or dropped from the design – they are the nice-to-haves on a requirements list.

The use of personas, goals and scenarios are powerful techniques that help to focus the product thinking even further.

Implications for technology management

This product mindset has implications for technology management because as we know many technologies, including IT systems have been developed with little or no regard for the person who was going to use it. It may have been possible to contain this in the past, but now it is just too visible. Technology, and especially software, is increasingly used by a wider and wider audience. This means that as organizations come to rely on technology more and more, they must ensure that it is fit for purpose and adds the value expected of it. As long as technology's performance, reliability and cost fall below customer needs, the market-place will dominated by early adopters: those who want (not need) the technology and who will pay a high price to get it. But the vast majority of customers are late adopters. They hold off until the technology has proven itself, and they insist upon convenience, good user experience and value.

This has implications for those organizations that implement unusable software that fails to live up to performance requirements, crashes or responds with incomprehensible error messages. If any of the late adopters use this software, they will only use it once before they go elsewhere. It is essential therefore that technology projects consider their primary end-user to be a late adopter and design the software solution so it meets their needs. In other words, develop precise personas of the users. You may not satisfy the technophile, but then, who cares; there are plenty of companies that do.

The next thing that the smart organization needs to do to ensure they manage their technology effectively is to ensure they manage their technology projects with care.

SMART
PEOPLE
TO HAVE
ON YOUR
SIDE

Geoffrey Moore

- President of the Chasm Group.
- Author of *Crossing the Chasm*.
- Believes the fundamental issue that has to be addressed in high-tech marketing is the ability to transition from an early market dominated by a few technical visionaries to one that is mainstream and dominated by pragmatists.

5

Smart Thinking IV – Manage Your Technology Projects with Care

Project management is a process that spans the full lifecycle of a project from inception to completion. Its cornerstone tenets are planning, execution and control of all resources, tasks and activities necessary to complete the project. In the end, project management is about people and process – how work is being performed.

Jim Johnson

Some of the worst excesses with technology occur within projects. Despite the criticality of IT to organizations, many experience immense difficulties in getting it to work. Ever since IT entered the vocabulary of the organization, a significant number of projects have either failed or delivered a sub-standard product. In addition, many of the benefits that heralded the introduction of huge, enterprise-wide systems have failed to materialize. Smart organizations not only know this, but they also do their best to manage their technology projects with care.

The critical role of the project manager

One of the key roles within a technology project is the project manager. Project management is a vital skill and the first stage to getting it right is to ensure that you have the right person running it. It is ironic that in most organizations, project management is considered vital but most project managers receive little or no training prior to taking on their role. Moreover, most organizations assume, quite wrongly, that someone can be plucked from the operational line and made into a project manager overnight. Not only does a project manager have a very different mindset to an operational manager but first-class project managers are hard to come by. What is of greater concern is that first-class technology project managers are particularly scarce. There are, unfortunately, many projects being run today by what I call the Titanic project manager. This is the person, who at the first sign of trouble, will leave their post in order to tackle an interesting technical problem. As captain, their job is to steer the project through the usually turbulent waters, not to manage technical issues. As soon as they leave their post, there is a real danger that the

> **Smart things to say**
>
> First-class technology products are delivered by first-class project managers

project will run into difficulties because there is no one leading it. This is, or course, not the only reason why they might fail, but given the complexities that have to be managed on a typical technology project, this behaviour is particularly damaging because it detracts away from the constant vigilance required to make it a success. Understanding how to make technology projects succeed in part depends on understanding why they fail. Here are some of the more common reasons:

- Insufficient user involvement

- Lack of senior management/executive support

- Ambiguous requirements – either poorly articulated, poorly captured, or just plain incomplete

- Poor up-front planning

- Planning to catch up

- Unrealistic expectations

- No project ownership

- Unclear, unambiguous objectives, vision and goals

- Incompetent staff

- Unrealistic project expectations

- Inappropriate, or non-existent risk management

- Severely compressed schedules – either imposed, or overly optimistic

- Poor communication

- Inappropriate productivity expectations

- Generally poor project management

- Concentration on the technological issues at the expense of the organizational

Westpac Bank (how not to do it)

When the Australian banking system was deregulated in 1984, the existing banks were forced to take a hard look at the way they did business because deregulation meant invasion by foreign banks. It also meant increased opportunities to compete locally and globally. Westpac saw information technology, and lots of it, as the weapon that would allow it to do so. Its high profile entry into the electronic financial services sector was called Core Systems 90 (CS90), and when it was publicly launched in August 1987, expectations were high. CS90 had an initial cost of around $A100 million and a completion date in the late 1980s, but in 1992, still two years from completion and $A50 million over budget, the project was terminated and 500 employees sacked. At its height the CS90 project involved 300 IT staff with a salary and overheads bill approaching $A1 million a month (Coleman, 1992; Kennedy, 1992).

CS90 was always a very ambitious project which at its core was a suite of five applications and a set of development tools. The idea was that the applications and the development tools would be proved in-house and then sold world-wide. From a technical perspective, CS90 was always feasible. Westpac had problems, however, in adapting its corporate culture to the demands of CS90, and although the initial marketing of CS90 to staff went well, it was not sustained. At first staff were enthusiastic about the potential benefits, but once the development staff started to delve into the costs of individual bank products the relationship broke down because of politics and the feeding of incorrect data to the development staff by the user communities. The IT staff also had major problems in trying to simultaneously create an in-house system as well as a commercially viable product for which there was an obvious global market.

So how can you recognize the first-class technology project manager? I believe the following are good indicators:

- First and foremost they must have a good grounding in project management, its associated skills and disciplines.

- They must have a sensitivity for the organizational and behavioural dimensions of the project not just the technical.

- They should understand the business benefits of technology.

- They must be capable of motivating the team and wider stakeholder community through strong leadership, personal action, passion and enthusiasm.

- They must have a strong personal presence and the ability to earn respect.

- They should be capable of adapting their craft to the organizational circumstances, rather than relying too heavily on a single method or methodology.

When it comes to delivering the project, the project manager must be able to apply their skills professionally, which means having a focus on the following aspects:

Planning

This means investing sufficient time in planning the project, and not leaping straight into the scheduling tool (such as Microsoft Project). Planning is more than just creating a Gantt chart, it involves determining what the project is to achieve, what it is going to produce, what techniques and tools it is to apply, and what resources it requires to achieve these. This is not an overnight pro-

KILLER QUESTIONS

Just how good a project manager are you?

cess, and nor is it something that the project manager should do in isolation. Engaging the project team and wider stakeholder community during the planning process can provide many benefits not least the commitment to the estimates.

Monitoring, control and visibility

Once started, the project has to be monitored and controlled. This typically involves managing the plan, the project's resources (people and money) and the constraints under which the project is executed – usually time, money and quality. Ensuring this is visible to the project stakeholders is very important. Visibility, however, is not about distributing the Gantt chart. In general, the Gantt is only designed to serve the project manager and their immediate team, as it allows the tasks and their duration to be tracked. Visibility, however, is about ensuring the mechanism, be it primarily graphical, or data based, allows the project's status and prognosis to be clearly understood by all stakeholders.

Communication

Communication is the lifeblood of any project. It has to be continuous and depends to a great extent on the project manager. Uncommunicative project managers, who are unwilling to talk to their team or their project stakeholders, are a significant danger. Communication at team level should be daily, and the adoption of a 15-minute meeting at the start of each working day can be beneficial. This meeting is especially useful during times of intense activity, such as when the project nears completion. Equally, having one-to-one meetings with the principal stakeholders is a must, as these can highlight potential areas of difficulty, especially associated with politics or power. It also allows some of the private views about the project to be fed back to the project manager

Benefits

As we saw in Chapter 3, too many projects fail to deliver any significant benefits, and even when they do they are usually significantly below those anticipated at the time of the business case. Being able to report on the status of the project from a benefits perspective is a valuable addition to project reporting, and demonstrates to senior management that the project manager is concerned about the outcomes of the project, and not just the project itself.

Power and politics

Many project managers shy away from power and politics because they believe they are difficult to manage, or feel that it is unimportant – as long as they deliver the project everything will be fine. There is plenty of evidence to suggest the opposite is true, as major projects involve a varying degree of power and politics. Being attuned to this, and managing it in a sensitive way allows the project manager to steer the project through the politics that will inevitably occur.

Guarding against the Mastermind project – I've started so I'll finish

One of the biggest traps with a technology project is over-commitment. This relates to the inability to stop a major initiative even when it is failing. The smart organization should recognize the warning signs and act accordingly, as otherwise they might end up spending vast amounts of money on a technology project that delivers them nothing but a large hole in their accounts. This type of problem is not just restricted to technology projects as it is often found in investment banks when traders try to trade their way out of a loss. Many find it difficult to take a loss and

Jeffery Pinto

- World expert on project management.
- Author of numerous books and articles, covering every aspect of project management from planning to teamwork.
- His research on successful and unsuccessful projects found that success depends on the following ten critical success factors:

  1. Project mission. The mission (or objective) of the project should be clear, unambiguous, and regularly communicated to all project stakeholders.

  2. Top management support. The continuous support of senior executives during the life of the project is a vital ingredient if it is to succeed.

  3. Planning. Proper planning is always a prerequisite for successful project delivery.

  4. Client consultation. Essentially actively involving the users and all other key stakeholders throughout the project.

  5. Personnel. Ensuring the appropriate use of competent expert resources (both technology and business) is vital.

  6. Technical tasks. The correct functioning of the technology itself, together with the technical work required to make it effective from a systems perspective.

  7. Client acceptance. The creation of the initial reception strategy for the project, as well as working with the ultimate users/client of the system to ensure ultimate acceptance.

  8. Monitoring and feedback. This involves maintaining a view of progress, and taking appropriate action when progress is at variance with the plan.

  9. Communication. Continuous communication with the principal stakeholders to ensure they are fully aligned with the project, and remain so as the project progresses.

  10. Troubleshooting. Dealing with the unexpected – after all, you cannot plan for everything.

instead hang onto losers. Unfortunately, a loss of 10 per cent requires a gain of more than 11 per cent to get even and a loss of 50 per cent requires a gain of 100 per cent. Therefore without some kind of risk management mechanism such problems can, in extreme cases, lead to the failure of an entire bank as we saw with Nick Leeson and Barings. Similarly, without the effective management of risk within the technology project, failure can be a very real outcome. The foundation of escalation lies in the irrational behaviours of individuals, which can be viewed at three distinct levels – the individual, the group and the senior executive. This extra level is especially dangerous because the positional power of the senior executive allows the intensity of the irrational behaviours to be amplified. Although it can be argued that the behaviours identified at this level are equally applicable to the individual, it is power that makes these behaviours more damaging.

People accountable for a failed decision find themselves caught in a no-win situation: some failure is inventible, but their superiors do not tolerate failure. Individuals in such a bind have but two options: own up, or cover up. Choosing to own up makes the day of atonement today; choosing a cover-up makes it tomorrow or perhaps never. Put in this bind, people seldom own up to failures and delay the day of atonement as long as possible. Several actions of deception are necessary to put things off. Offsetting bad news with good news deflects potentially threatening questions. The cover-up is two-tiered: the distorted good news and the blatant act of creating misleading information. These games of deception become "undiscussable" because to reveal them would also reveal the lose-lose position created for the organization.

Paul Nutt

Individual behaviour

There are four behaviours that can lead us as individuals to behave irrationally. These are:

- *Availability error*. The most recent material is "available". Previous knowledge and data is lost in the immediacy of the event. Not surprisingly, this type of irrational behaviour is often stimulated by dramatic events.

- *Halo effect*. The tendency to see all personal attributes consistently. For example, a good sportsman is expected to be a good businessman, father, indeed good at everything. This can equally work in the reverse, where someone is classed as being a general all round poor performer.

- *Primacy error*. Beliefs formed by first impressions, with later evidence interpreted in light of this initial impression. The adage that first impressions count is applicable here and if powerful, primacy error can generate positive or negative halo effects early on within a relationship.

- *Conformity error*. Individual conformance to the behaviour of others whether they know they are making a mistake by doing so, or whether they are unaware both of their mistake and of the social pressure that has induced them to make it.

Group behaviour

Whereas individual behaviour can be controlled, when irrational behaviours manifest themselves with groups and particularly project teams, the situation can become unmanageable. There are two forms:

- *Group bias*. Where group members' attitudes are biased in one direction, the interaction of the group will tend to increase this bias because of the need to be valued and suppress criticism. Engaging in a common task only decreases hostility between groups if the outcome is successful. Where it is not, blame is passed from one group to the other, with any existing divisions widening.

• *Stereotypes.* Stereotypes are convenient tools for assessing an individual who belongs to a group. As a result, rather than expected to act individually, a member of a group is expected to conform to the stereotypical behaviour of the entire group. Therefore, no attempt is made at assessing an individual's behaviour in isolation from the rest of the group. Stereotypes tend to be self-fulfilling because of both primacy and availability errors.

Senior executive behaviour

Finally we reach the red zone of irrationality, where the mix of power and status can result in some of the strongest forms of irrational behaviour. There are four behaviours that we have to guard against:

• *Public decisions.* Public decisions are more likely to be executed than those taken privately. In general, people do not want to lose face, especially in public. This is a classic problem with government-sponsored projects.

• *Misplaced consistency.* Someone who has embarked on a course of action may feel they must continue to justify their initial decision. People who have made a sacrifice – time, effort or money – in order to do something, tend to go on doing it even when they stand to lose more than they could gain by continuing. There is always the hope that the situation can be retrieved.

- *Ignoring the evidence.* People tend to seek confirmation of their current hypothesis whereas they should be trying to disprove it. In general, there is a refusal to look for contradictory evidence or, indeed believe or act upon it if it is brought to one's attention.

- *Distorting the evidence.* Evidence favouring a belief will strengthen it while contradictory evidence is ignored. As a result the belief remains intact. Therefore, when faced with evidence that is contrary to a particular viewpoint this evidence will be distorted and dismissed as being irrelevant or inapplicable. Where the evidence is partially correct, it will be distorted to emphasize the positive aspects over the negative.

SMART
PEOPLE
TO HAVE
ON YOUR
SIDE

Helga Drummond

- Professor of Decision Sciences at the University of Liverpool, UK.
- Author of eight books, including *Escalation in Decision Making* and *The Art of Decision Making*.
- Shows how to avoid over-commitment to a failing course of action (which includes projects).

According to Mark Keil (2000), there are seven ways to de-escalate commitment to a failing project:

1. Don't ignore negative feedback or external pressure.

2. Hire an external auditor to provide a more objective assessment.

3. Don't be afraid to withhold further funding.

4. Look for opportunities to redefine the problem.

5. Manage impressions.

6. Prepare your stakeholders.

7. Look for opportunities to de-institutionalize the project.

Another way is to assess the risks of escalation by reviewing the technology project against the following criteria:

- The imposition of tight and, unrealistic timescales. This includes those imposed by the organization on their internal IT department or external vendor, those that are self-imposed by a third-party technology supplier in order to win the contract, or those that are the result of external market pressure – such as a sudden change in the economic climate, or the need to address regulatory requirements.

- The need for significant capital and non-capital investment.

- The expectation of significant returns on investment. This might be imposed by the organization through investment appraisal hurdle rates, expected because of one or two high-profile and well-publicized successes, or stated as achievable by a third-party supplier wanting to win the business.

- The use of leading-edge technologies (or technologies that are at the boundary of an organization's capability), to break into new markets, or to introduce major organizational change.

- Where the future of the business depends on the successful outcome of the project, or the project is considered business critical. Such projects typically have to succeed, no matter what the cost.

- Where the careers of senior managers depend on the successful outcome of the project.

- Where the project has been publicly announced, either within the organization, to the wider business population, or in the case of government projects, the general population.

If you assess your project against each of these and can say yes to more than half you are likely to be embarking on (or perhaps already in them midst of) a project that may be prone to escalation. If you are, then it is vital that you monitor people's behaviour very carefully to spot any obvious signs of over-commitment.

Actively manage your risks

Smart technology management requires the organization to be good at managing the risks associated with implementation. This is not just about managing the project related risks as it also extends into managing the investment and financial risks associated with any technology project (see Chapter 2). The process through which project risks are identified, managed and controlled involves a continuous process that has the following four steps:

1. *Identification.* The process of identifying risks will vary according to its nature. Whereas most financial risks are identified using sophisticated models, operational and project risks require more qualitative approaches, such as structured thinking, brainstorming, scenario analysis and so on.

2. *Quantification.* The process of quantification involves evaluating each risk (or a collection of risks, where they interact) to determine the impact and the likelihood of them materializing. Again, there are various tools to help, such as simulations, decision tree analysis use of experts and so on.

3. *Response development.* Although every identified risk needs a response, those that have only a limited impact may be allowed to follow their course because the costs of avoiding them may outweigh their impacts. When developing a response a number of

options are open to the risk manager. Risks can be avoided by taking actions to ensure they pose no threat at all, although this may mean taking an entirely different path in the investment, business or programme/project. If they cannot be avoided, action can be taken to reduce either the impact or likelihood. And if all else fails, some form of contingency plan can be developed that allows the risk to be dealt with once it has matured. For example, the risks posed by the Year 2000 date change were managed through a combination of reduction and avoidance strategies. This involved retiring old hardware, changing software to cope with the change in date and developing sophisticated contingency plans that involved hiring power generators, central banks providing increased liquidity in the markets and governments having emergency services on standby

---

Eddie Obeng

- Managing director of Pentacle, the virtual business school.
- Author of a number of books on project management, including *All Change: The Project Leader's Secret Handbook*.
- Believes that there are four basic types of technology project, each imposing different levels of risk and each requiring a different execution approach:
    1. Quest – the business knows what it wants, but the technologists don't know what to do to achieve it.
    2. Fog – the business does not really know what it wants and the technologists do not know how they are going to achieve it.
    3. Movie – the business does not know what is wants but the technologists know how to build it; whatever it is (often the case of a technical solution looking for a problem).
    4. Painting by numbers – the business knows what it wants and the technologists know how to build it.

SMART
PEOPLE
TO HAVE
ON YOUR
SIDE

4. *Monitor and control*. Risks are rarely static and because they are associated with future events there will come a time when they will either mature or no longer pose a threat. This requires the organization to ensure there is appropriate ownership for their management and that all risks are suitably monitored to assess any change in their status.

Beware, but don't ignore politics

In politics you must always keep running with the pack. The moment that you falter and they sense that you are injured, the rest will turn on you like wolves.

R. A. Butler

Many people dismiss organizational politics as irrelevant and certainly do not believe it to be as underhand as that associated with government circles. However, the truth is that it is more like the pure variant of politics than we give it credit for. But before we can discuss politics we need to outline the difference between power and politics:

• Power in its simplest form is the influence one person has over another to get things done. Power is about inequalities, ownership of resources in its various forms, and control.

• Politics is perceived to be the illegitimate use of power for personal means. Politics circumvents the legitimate power that resides in organizations and is a way of gaining power through means other than those prescribed by the organization.

Given that technology projects exacerbate inter-functional rivalries and involve at least some disruption in the balance of power, it should come as no surprise that there will be political manoeuvring as they are executed. So although organizations have realized that projects are the most effective means of introducing radical, and rapid change, they come at a price – politics.

There are three underlying reasons why politics exists within organizations (Egan, 1994):

- *Competition for scarce or prized resources.* This includes physical resources such as equipment and office space as well as human capital, position and status. It is not uncommon to see political problems arise within projects that require the same skilled resource as the operational line, nor is it surprising to see arguments and backstabbing associated with roles, responsibilities and positions within organizations. In both circumstances, there would be no politics if resources were in abundant supply or there was no competition for positions of power.

- *Self-interest.* Although there are many people within enterprises who place organizational interests above their own, there are a significant minority who will pursue a path of self-interest. This may mean them appearing to do the right thing for the organization, but it usually masks ulterior motives. Such self-interest should not be overlooked within a project, and if anything, it should be surfaced as quickly as possible and actively addressed.

- *Power and the struggle to achieve it.* The feeling of having no power is unbearable to the majority of people and where a project is altering the balance of power, a political reaction should be expected. Interestingly, nothing has really changed since the times of the medieval court. Here the courtiers had to be elegant, committed and friendly, while scheming and plotting in the background. Overt power plays were frowned upon and could end up in imprisonment or death.

Today the same rules apply, people must appear civilized, decent, democratic and fair, but none of us can take these rules too literally, as we will be crushed by those who are plotting around us. Therefore it is naïve to expect the full commitment and buy-in from all stakeholders during the project. Just because they are spending large sums of money on the project does not mean that everyone believes in what it is hoping to achieve.

SMART
PEOPLE
TO HAVE
ON YOUR
SIDE

Gerard Egan

- Professor of Organization Development and Psychology at Loyala University, Chicago.
- Author of *Working the Shadow Side*.
- Shows how to use behind-the-scenes management to get things done.
- Describes how we can practice politics.

In order to manage politics it is first necessary to identify and analyse it. This can be achieved using the following four steps (Egan, 1994):

1. Identify the activities and actions that are associated with the organization's scarce or prized resources

Political infighting typically occurs around such things as change projects, technology investments, research and development and product development. Increasingly, the reduction in the number of senior management positions within organizations has led to much higher stakes between those who seek the trappings of power. As a result there is significantly more political infighting between those who wish to become the senior managers of the future. Once the sources of political battles have been identified it is necessary to identify everyone who is involved, as this will help to frame the extent of the political landscape that has to be managed.

2. Identify the motivations behind competitive activities

Successfully managing politics requires the identification of the motivations of those involved. The creation of a stakeholder map that identifies the key relationships, rivalries and alliances of those touched by the project is a key activity.

3. Identify the sources of power

Power resides in five fundamental forms:

- Positional power which is the legitimized power that exists in a person's position within an organization.

- Status power that exists by virtue of the title people are given, even when they have no real positional power. For example, non-executive directors would fall into this category.

- Resource power resides in anyone who manages or owns scarce resource (money, people and so on).

- Veto – the power to say no. It is important not to ignore this as even people who are low down in the organization have the ability to say no, especially when they control resources.

- Expertise. The guru or subject matter expert can be a powerful figure in any organization.

4. Assess the political strategies adopted by those who seek power or control scarce resources

For completeness, I have included some of the common political strategies used within organizations (Table 5.1; see Simmons, 1998). It should be remembered, of course, that these political behaviours are essentially about power, either its acquisition or retention. They are especially important within the context of a technology project because of the damage they can cause. Valuable time can be wasted on trying to gain buy-in from reluctant functional units, seeking out vital information, or gaining access to senior managers. All of these sap the project's energy, and, of course are usually deliberate moves to limit its progress.

Robert Green
- Award-winning journalist.
- Author of *The 48 Laws of Power*.
- Believes that you ignore power at your peril.

No more project heroics – or what to do if things don't go according to plan

Project heroics occur when the project team realizes that it will not deliver the technology in time and decides to embark on a course of action that results in them working inhuman hours, burning out and ruining any chance of delivering the project. It is far better to be level headed about the problems that do occur and take the advice of Steve McConnell (1996) who believes that following the actions set out below can bring a late-running project back on track.

Table 6.1 Political behaviours

Political behaviour	Description
Ownership	An individual or group owns a project, product line, department, process and benefit from the status and rights of ownership. Ownership is all about control by being there first. Within projects, it is the ownership of resources that typically creates the greatest amount of political turbulence.
Information manipulation	Knowledge is power. More information generates more filters through which it must pass. And each filter provides ample opportunity for information distortion. Typical tactics include withholding information and manipulating it to change the message (for example distorting bad news to appear good, or not divulging it). Information manipulation is increasingly linked to ownership.
Alliances	Political battles within organizations usually involves taking sides. Types of behaviour include those associated with sycophants, sleepers (waiting to join the winning side), shoulder rubbers (face to face contacts), and those that monopolize other people's time.
Invisible walls	This is especially applicable to projects where rules, procedures and information access are placed in its path to slow it down, derail it and generally prevent it from achieving its objectives. The invisible wall game is best played by those who can maintain the appearance of sincere effort, but without actually achieving anything.
Strategic non-compliance	Agreeing up front to co-operate, and default on the agreement at the last minute, leaving little or no opportunity for the other party to do anything about it.
Discrediting	It is said that reputation is one of the cornerstones of power, and once lost is almost impossible to regain. Therefore, discrediting individuals is one of the surest ways to gain power.
Camouflage	The purpose of camouflage is to distract or confuse people long enough to defuse or deflect a course of action. This type of behaviour would usually result in the project team hunting down needless information, at the project's expense. Camouflage can sometimes be associated with discrediting.

Jane Clarke

- Director of the business psychology consultancy Nicholson McBride.
- Author of *Office Politics: A Survival Guide.*
- Helps to identify your political challenges and offers tangible strategies for handling every political situation you may encounter.

- Fix the parts of the development process that are not working. This includes the standard project management and software development activities such as risk and issue management, configuration management, planning, reporting and testing

- Create detailed milestones for the remainder of the project. Focusing the project on short-term deliverables is vital, so that control can be re-established. A new schedule linking these milestones and those associated with the remainder of the project together should also be created. This will provide an indication of how long the activities will take to complete, and highlight the dependencies between them.

- Make these milestones visible, and ensure that they are reported against at least every week, and where required, more frequently. As well as detailing achievements, the report should also include reasons why milestones have been missed. This will establish trends. For example, if the milestones are consistently missed by individual team members it would suggest that the productivity assumptions made during the initial planning were incorrect. In revising these assumptions, there will be a subsequent impact on the schedule, as additional time will be required to complete the remaining work.

- Stabilize and freeze the requirements, especially if these have been changing frequently during the project.

- Consider reducing the functionality. If this is necessary, it is best to link the functionality to the benefits. Cutting functionality where there is little or no benefit is a good starting point. One way to achieve this is to link any cuts back to the scenarios discussed in the previous chapter. Removing any of the daily use scenarios would be the wrong thing to do, but removing functionality associated with edge scenarios would.

- Remove any functionality that is of poor quality.

- Monitor and control the number of defects by tracking and tackling them through stringent code reviews.

- Maintain regular communication with the project's stakeholder community, and ensure they are fully aware of progress and issues as they arise.

- Try not to add more staff to the project, as this will lead to a lengthening of project schedule – one of the classic Brooks' laws (see Smart People to have on your side). Care should also be taken where staff are to be removed from the team because of poor performance. Before doing so, it is recommended the impact on the remainder of

---

Fred Brooks
- Author of *The Mythical Man Month*.
- Recognized there were no magic bullets that would improve software development.
- Developed principles of software project management that are as applicable today as when the book was first written, over 25 years ago.

SMART
PEOPLE
TO HAVE
ON YOUR
SIDE

the team be gauged, as such an action may have significant, and negative repercussions on morale and productivity.

- Once the project has completed, conduct a post mortem to assess why its performance deviated. This should be used to draw out any changes that have to be made to the project management and software development processes and fed into future projects.

Advice to the smart technology project manager

Here are some things that the smart technology project manager should do to ensure that they, and their projects, are successful:

- Commit to applying best-practice project management techniques throughout the project. Getting the basics right will go a long way to achieving an effective outcome.

- Where historical project data exists (project size, budgeted costs, actual costs at completion, baseline schedule, actual schedule at completion, benefits achieved, and so on) use these to aid in the planning of your project. Where they do not exist, start collecting them, and share them amongst the wider project community.

- Understand the dynamics of large projects, particularly over-commitment. If you can see the warning signs in yourself, then you will be able to see them in others.

- When a project is escalating out of control, do something about it before it is too late.

- Don't pay lip-service to business involvement, and ensure your communication skills are up to par.

- When discussing the merits of a new system with the business, avoid using technical jargon. Put yourself in the business professional's shoes and talk in their language.

- When discussing sponsorship for the project, focus on the benefits first.

- Make the project's progress visible, and easy to interpret. Make reporting simple and focused; there should be only four things management should need to know about your project – have you completed what you said you would when you would, have you spent what you expected to spend, will you complete the project on time, to budget and will it provide the organization with the benefits promised in the business case?

- When progress has deviated from the plan, understand why this is the case. If it is a random problem make sure it does not happen again. If it is a systematic problem, revisit the plan. But, whatever you do, make sure the slippage is visible and its impacts known.

- Never believe you and the project team can make up for lost time. Once time is lost, it is lost for good, and project heroics do no one any favours in the long run. It reduces productivity and increases the likelihood of errors.

- Be honest if the project is going off the rails. Honesty early on can allow most situations to be rectified, and provide sufficient time to consider the alternatives.

- Use the five project outcomes (the project runs to time, budget and delivers all that is expected of it; the project is late/over budget but delivers all that is expected of it; the project is on time and to budget but has been descoped to meet these two constraints; the project is late/over budget and delivers a reduced functionality; the project fails) as a visibility tool. Assess the probability of each of these outcomes at regular intervals and use it as an additional tool to manage and report on the project.

- Recognize that politics within technology projects includes the dimension of information. With less opportunity for the attainment of positional and status power, people will look to information as a source of power. Being able to broker between opposing camps will be an important skill in the future. Therefore understand the principles of win–win negotiations

- Ensure that adequate time is given to testing the software. If the schedule is slipping, do not compress the time allocated to testing. Failing to test software thoroughly can have major, and very expensive implications.

- Remember the value of thinking in terms of products.

- Track the benefits of the project meticulously both during the project, and once it has completed. You may not believe this is part of your job, but it is, and success is down to your ability to work with the business to help them understand their role in delivering the benefits.

- Ensure you have the correct mix of technical and business skills within the project team, and consider the team's capabilities when drawing together the plan and making the estimates.

- Always ensure the team are aware of the bigger picture and keep them up to date with overall status of the project.

Project management is an essential component to smart technology management. Without it, no technology product would ever reach the market and no system would ever be implemented. Despite its significance to technology management, very few companies take the trouble to nurture and develop their project management talent. In today's competitive markets, those who have excellent project management will succeed. But, in order to manage technology effectively, the smart organization must also be smart at reception strategies – making sure that the customers and users actually want to use the technology when they have it.

6

Smart Thinking V – Reception Strategies Matter

> With so much at stake, the erratic results of high-tech marketing are particularly frustrating, especially in a society where other forms of marketing appear to be so well under control.
>
> Geoffrey Moore

There is little point in investing in new technology if those who are expected to use it can't or won't. Thus an essential part of smart technology management is ensuring that people will use the technology when it has been implemented. Although obvious to say, this means focusing on people and technology. Unfortunately there is a tendency to

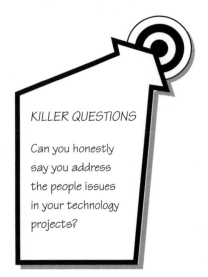

Can you honestly
say you address
the people issues
in your technology
projects?

focus on the latter at the expense of the former, and it is a sad fact that most projects address too narrow an agenda and have a too strong a focus on technology. What is equally sad is that the majority of organizations recognize they are poor at managing the people and organizational aspects of change and are just as bad at assessing the wider impacts of new technology. The smart organization understands this and will create a reception strategy that addresses these needs. In simple terms a reception strategy is designed to address the individual and collective requirements of those who will be using the technology. It is consists of three elements:

1. *The readiness to change assessment*, which is designed to assess the degree of change that will occur with the implementation of the new technology.

2. *The business transition plan*, which is the core component of the reception strategy. This covers the communication and stakeholder management dimensions of managing the change.

3. *Training*, which will include a training needs analysis as well as the execution of the training itself.

The reception strategy begins before the project is started. A common mistake is to consider it just before implementation, which is fatal and leads to an unnecessary drop in productivity. The reception strategy is important because it addresses the typical issues faced when dealing with any change, particularly resistance. It is well known that the sooner people are engaged in the change process, the sooner they will understand and come to terms with it.

Creating the reception strategy involves the following steps:

1. Understand what you are dealing with, especially in relation to resistance to change and expectation management.

2. Assess the stakeholders and determine what they want to achieve from the new technology.

3. Create the business transition plan for managing the stakeholders and their expectations, including assessing their readiness to change and identifying their communication needs.

4. Link the business transition plan to the overall project plan and work closely with the stakeholder community to introduce the new technology smoothly.

Step 1 – understand what you are dealing with

The first step in developing any reception strategy is to understand the pitfalls that will have to be avoided. This will involve learning from previous technology implementations (successful and unsuccessful) and learning from the experts. It also means understanding the nature of resistance to change and recognizing that when It comes to new technology, changes in productivity are rarely immediate. This last point is crucial because virtually all technology projects are sold on the basis of improving productivity.

Learning from experts is a great way to avoid the pitfalls of technology failure, although it is critical that you determine which issues are applicable to your own organization rather than taking the factors at face value. This means reviewing your organization's past projects, both successful and unsuccessful, and drawing out those factors that may impact your current project. Once known, it is useful to update the processes through which technology is implemented as this will help you to maintain a successful track record. The two areas that require some further analysis are resistance to change and expectation management.

Resistance to change

There are many technology projects that seem to fail at the very last hurdle of implementation. The project appeared to have all the support necessary to allow it to succeed, and yet, just as it was about to complete, it was rejected, and terminated (see the EasyJet example in Chapter 1). Although the reasons for its rejection are often wrapped up in technical reasons, much can be put down to the political manoeuvring of key stakeholders who may employ the strategic non-compliance game (see Chapter 5). At this point in the project, there is very little one can do.

It is useful to understand that successful change depends on a number of factors, including:[1]

- *Structure*. Most organizations have a well-defined structure with established rules and procedures which are designed to maintain the status quo. Depending on the flexibility of such structures, the ability to change will vary significantly. For example, very rigid hierarchical structures are more likely to resist change than those which are more loosely structured.

- *Culture*. Some organizations have very rigid cultures, themselves partly created and reinforced through structure. These tend to be very adept at resisting change, or providing the illusion of change when in reality they have not changed at all. This is particularly true of bureaucratic organizations, such as government bodies. There are

[1]Brown (1995). For a general discussion on change, and resistance to change, see Moss Kanter (1983).

also those cultures that exist which are sufficiently flexible to cope with continuous and radical change. This is typical of the high technology sector. Culture is an important factor that should not be overlooked

> **Smart things to say**
>
> If you want your radical change to succeed, do what Cortez did: burn your boats

- *Individual habit.* Individuals and groups within organizations prefer routine – it provides comfort and allows them to develop competence. It also creates a sense of community within the local working environment, which is something that can benefit the function and organization as a whole. When this environment changes, the comfort provided by habit, routine and familiarity are disturbed, which often leads to resistance. Change involves breaking these comfortable habits and forcing people out of their comfort zone. As expected, no one likes significant change and to be successful requires plenty of communication, careful management and training.

- *Security.* It is paradoxical that, despite near record levels of employment in the United States and the United Kingdom, people feel very insecure. It is believed this insecurity stems from the general economic turbulence, the throw-back from the downsizing experience of the early 1990s and the continuous advances in computer technology. Insecurity can breed resistance, as the fear of being downsized is a great motivator for entrenchment. It also limits the creativity of organizations, as employees believe that taking risks exposes them to personal failure, and the sack. The downsizing in the 1990s also diminished the trust between employees and their employers, thereby reinforcing the view that it is better to commit to oneself than to an employer who will eliminate headcount at the slightest hint of a market downturn

Spencer Johnson and Kenneth Blanchard

- Authors of the best-selling book *Who Moved My Cheese*.
- Demonstrated the value of embracing and enjoying change.

- *Power, status and esteem.* As mentioned in the previous chapter, projects will by their very nature upset the balance of power within an organization. Therefore, when a change is perceived to affect a person's power base, they will do all they can to protect what they have. Of course, there will be those who see the project as an ideal opportunity to gain power, and so will do all they can to ensure it succeeds. The key is to watch out for the counter-champion who can be a powerful enemy in any major change initiative.

Resistance to change in relation to new technology is not, therefore, a simple rejection of a proposed, or newly implemented system. It is a complex combination of factors that can be organizational or individual, but primarily situational in nature. The strongly held belief that resistance to change is a phenomenon that needs to be eliminated by the project team is indicative of a technocentric mentality that puts technology before people in organizations. Resistance to change ought to be recognized as action – rather than reaction – and be seen as a way of conveying important messages to the project team. It should also be recognized as being a normal course of events for organizations, and particularly successful ones.

Expectation management

As we saw in Chapter 3, the majority of technology investments predict healthy and immediate gains in productivity, usually as soon as it is

David Firth

- Principal of the international consultancy Treefrog, which specializes in the psychology of change.
- International consultant, writer and conference speaker.
- Author of a number of books on people and change.
- Believes that the more we fight resistance, the more it will fight back.
- Asserts that change is not a battle, but about helping people adapt consciously from a status quo that no longer serves the company to a new world that will.
- States that resistance should be regarded as a sign that the desired change has begun and should be viewed as loyalty in action.

SMART
PEOPLE
TO HAVE
ON YOUR
SIDE

implemented. We have also seen that this is often not the case, because there is a reduction in performance when the new technology is introduced as staff are retrained. And, once implemented, there also tends to be a period of adjustment during which staff become familiar with the technology, come to terms with the subtle changes to business process that accompany it, and deal with performance issues such as bugs. It can therefore be some time before the existing level of performance is reached, let alone the predicted level (Figure 6.1). Thus, the improved performance levels on which the investment was based may take a lot longer to materialize than anticipated. The grey area of Figure 6.1 reflects the additional costs associated with this reduction in productivity. Managing expectations therefore extends to setting realistic productivity targets as the new technology beds in. Any costs associated with an expected dip in productivity that precedes and follows implementation should be accounted for in the business case. It is far better to be honest about the effects of the technology than paint a rosy picture of what could happen but probably won't. This helps to establish commit-

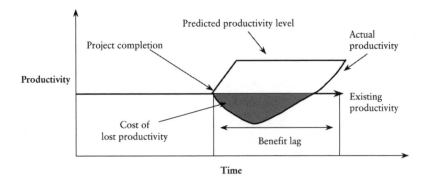

Figure 6.1 Performance and new investment.

ment from the principal stakeholders who are more likely to work with the project team if there is honesty about what the new technology can and cannot do. It also helps to avoid some of the problems of over-commitment (see Chapter 5).

Step 2 – Assess the stakeholders

Because people constitute the major barrier to change, it is critical that their needs and concerns are addressed early on in the project. The need to understand the stakeholders cannot be overstated because what we have found in any large undertaking is that you cannot treat people the same. There will be those who are extremely positive and look forward to the change, there will be the cynics, the fence-sitters, the agonistics and, of course, the hard-core elements who will resist. There are also other ways to view stakeholders. There are the senior executives, the managers and the staff who will have to deal with the technology on a daily basis. Understanding that every stakeholder group may require a different method of handling makes the reception strategy and its core component of the business transition plan much easier to produce and execute. There will, of course, be issues along the way, but you will be in a much better position to spot them before they occur.

Assessing stakeholders involves the following seven steps (Figure 6.2). Steps 1–5 relate to assessing the stakeholders; steps 6 and 7 refer to the reception strategy itself.

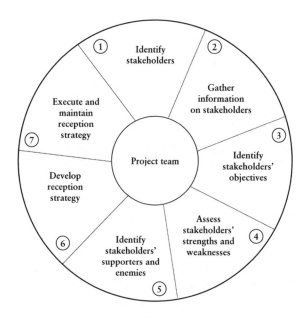

Figure 6.2 Assessing the stakeholders and creating the reception strategy.

[Adapted from Cleland's model of stakeholder management within projects. For a description of this model, see Cleland (1988).]

1. *Identify the stakeholders.* This will entail identifying those people within the organization that will have an interest in the project.

2. *Gather information on stakeholders.* As each stakeholder is identified, the following information should be collected:

   - their role(s)

   - their responsibilities

   - their position

   - their status

   - their sources of power (positional, status, knowledge, veto and expertise).

3. *Identify the stakeholder's objectives.* This means understanding what each stakeholder wants to achieve from the project. For many it will be a positive outcome, but it is important to recognize that the project will create imbalances in the organization. Therefore it is unlikely that all stakeholders will feel the same way and some may be extremely negative. The strategy will need to reflect this and these feelings should be tracked over time because stakeholders may well change their opinion about the project as it progresses. So, although some may view the project in a positive light to begin with, they may change their opinion as they realize what the outcome will mean for them personally (or their team, department or function). Any issues that arise from this will have to be addressed by the project team. It is also important to watch out for those who appear ambivalent and sit on the fence. These people will make their views known very late on in the project, often causing major disruption. The team should be aiming to smoke such people out as quickly as possible to ensure that the apparently neutral stakeholder's real feelings are known. Other stakeholders will be looking

for other outcomes including opportunities for promotions, and the resolution of power struggles. Understanding these drivers is essential to the reception strategy and will help frame how each stakeholder needs to be managed. The best way to understand this is to ask, as most stakeholders will be willing to state what they want. In essence it is about establishing each stakeholder's WIIFM (what's in it for me) and then working to meet these throughout the project.

4. *Assess stakeholders' strengths and weaknesses.* The reception strategy should take into account the relative strengths and weaknesses of each stakeholder. These can range from personal characteristics, such as emotional intelligence, persuasive ability, through to leadership characteristics, creditability, peer respect and so on. The purpose of this assessment is threefold. First, it is to identify the areas of weakness that may have to be covered by the project team. Second, it is to watch out for areas of risk within the relationship and help to predict the issues and manage them appropriately. And, third, it should determine which strengths should be played to and which ones can be employed by the project team to improve the likelihood of success

5. *Identify stakeholders' supporters and enemies.* No one is an island, and it would naïve to expect that everyone within an organization will get on well with everyone else all of the time. The purpose of this stage is to create a relationship map of the major links that exist between each of the identified stakeholders. Mapping these will allow the project team to understand how key stakeholders relate to each other. It is also very useful to plot each stakeholder's position in relation to the project (positive, negative or neutral). The example shown in Figure 6.3 suggests that the project team only has access to a small number of the stakeholders they need to manage. However,

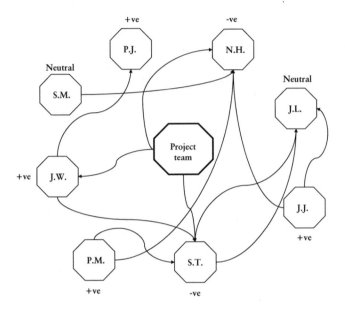

Figure 6.3 The relationship map.

by mapping the relationships between the stakeholders it is possible
to manage the relationship through one or more of the other stakeholders. In addition, it helps to understand how an individual
stakeholder's opinion of the project can be influenced by another.
This stage will also help to clarify some of the political issues that
are likely to affect the project as it progresses. The arrows within
Figure 6.3 represent the influence one stakeholder has over another,
and the +ve, -ve and neutral indicators above each represents their
feelings toward the project.

6. *Develop the reception strategy.* This will bring everything together
   for each of the key relationships that must be managed.

Kirkpatrick Sale

- Editor and author.
- Author of *Rebels Against the Future.*
- Believes that we can learn plenty from the nineteenth-century Luddite movement, including:
  1. Technologies are never neutral and some are hurtful.
  2. Industrialism is always a cataclysmic process, destroying the past, roiling the present and making the future uncertain.

Step 3 – develop the business transition plan

The real purpose of the business transition plan is to manage the process through which people cope with the change ahead of them. Despite the process being well known, it is surprising just how badly it is managed. In general, people will pass through the following five stages (Figure 6.4):

1. *Denial.* To begin with they will deny that anything is happening, believing it to be a short-term fad or passing management initiative (see Smart People to Have on Your Side: Petruska Clarkson).

2. *Resistance.* Once they realize that it is not a passing fad, they begin to resist, which for some might mean leaving their job while others will use politics to undermine the project.

3. *Choices.* Over time, and with sufficient communication and involvement in the project, they begin to see some alternatives and start to assess the other options and how they might adjust to the new environment.

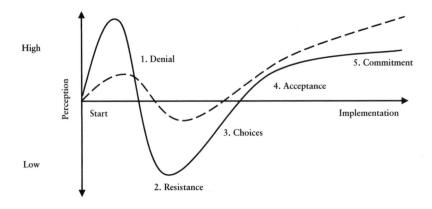

Figure 6.4 The change cycle.

4. *Acceptance.* The process of assessing and working out options begins to create acceptance to the change and they decide that the new world is better than the old.

5. *Commitment.* The final stage is commitment where they are keen to become involved with the change and help to make it happen.

This process will vary slightly for technology projects, as at the beginning there is usually wild enthusiasm for the new initiative, which after a while begins to wane as stakeholders begin to fall into the standard change process. The reception strategy is designed to reduce the extremes of emotion that usually accompanies change. To achieve this it is a good idea to address the bad messages as well as the good. All too often organizations avoid bad news which pushes it underground only to resurface at a later date –often when it is too late to do anything about it.

Communication is an essential and often overlooked aspect of manag-

Petruska Clarkson

- Consultant, chartered clinical counselling psychologist, counsellor, mentor and psychotherapist.
- Author of *Change in Organizations*.
- Believes there are five outcomes of change:
  - Real change – which everyone aims for, but few achieve.
  - No change – the status quo prevails.
  - Impossible change – just too hard or too fast to achieve, which leads to disillusionment.
  - Destructive change – leading to major fallout and problems with those expected to change.
  - Fake change – everything looks on the surface to have changed, but in reality nothing has.

SMART
PEOPLE
TO HAVE
ON YOUR
SIDE

ing the business transition. Organizations tend to opt for either no communication or blanket communiqués which fail to address the real issues. One of the purposes of undertaking the stakeholder analysis is to establish the communication needs of each stakeholder group and there are plenty of channels open to you, including:

- Face to face

- Email

- Company intranet

- Town hall meetings (where people can express opinions without come back)

- Newsletters

- Memos

- Presentations

- Briefings and cascaded briefings

The choice very much depends on the type of message that is to be con-

Carol Kinsey Gorman

- President of Kinsey Consulting Services and recognized expert on the human side of organizational change.

- Author of *The Human Side of High-tech*.

- Identified 16 change management lessons:

  1. Hire flexible, self motivated people who can cope with change.

  2. Involve people in the change.

  3. Watch out for complacency – this is a sign of a lack of challenge.

  4. Remember that everyone dislikes change.

  5. For change to be successful, know and communicate the "why".

  6. Lead people through change by demonstrating concern for them.

  7. Be flexible and where necessary adjust the change strategy.

  8. Ensure you communicate the big picture as well as what it means personally.

  9. Always communicate . . . there can never be too much.

  10. Ensure the business leaders embrace and lead the change.

  11. Give people the wider information they need to understand how the world is changing.

  12. Have fun during the process.

  13. Develop a culture of change acceptance.

  14. Address the emotional elements of change.

  15. Accept that change is never final.

  16. Be prepared for radical change.

veyed and the audience. If you are in any doubt, it is a good idea to ask the stakeholders what their preferences are.

One thing that often helps with communication is identifying and recruiting project champions from within the community that will be expected to change. Because such people are passing through the same process, their views are more likely to be accepted. They can become important channels for managing the major messages around the technology and are essential sources of intelligence. According to Jeffery Pinto (1994), the champion will need to take on each of the following roles:

KILLER QUESTIONS

Do you have change masters in your project teams?

- *Cheerleader* – providing motivation.

- *Visionary* – maintaining the sense of purpose.

- *Politician* – dealing with the politics of change.

- *Risk taker* – being willing to take personal risks in order to make the project a success.

- *Ambassador* – keeping the stakeholder community cohesive.

Champions are a great way to prepare the ground for implementation but they have to be picked with care. Indeed, sometimes it is better to have a converted cynic than an evangelist as a champion because they are more likely to earn the respect of their peers more readily.

The final aspect to business transition is training. Training is one of the biggest wins you can get with technology projects, but is so often cut because of schedule pressure. For training to be successful it is necessary to undertake a training needs analysis. This involves assessing the indi-

It is better to have allies when implementing change, so seek out and recruit champions who can work alongside you and the project team

vidual needs for training, or if the end-user community is much larger, the collective needs. The specific needs can be derived from the gap between current processes and working patterns and those that will exist when the new technology has been implemented. It is important to include process and role changes as well as the more obvious technology changes within this analysis. The outcome of the training needs analysis will feed into the design and execution of the training.

Step 4 – linking the business transition plan to the project plan

The output of business transition planning is the creation of a plan with defined actions and milestones. For this plan to be useful and effective it must be integrated into the other activities of the project and managed appropriately.

This concludes the core elements of smart technology management. But to be truly smart, there are three other aspects that must be mastered:

1. How to manage the technology we already have (Chapter 7).

2. How to ensure IT has board level presence (Chapter 8).

3. How to keep ahead of the game (Chapter 9).

7

How Should We Manage Technology?

The Nasdaq may rise and fall. Dot-coms will come and go. But there is no doubt that anyone in business today will be managing technology of many sorts. It doesn't matter whether you work in fast foods, museums, hospitals, or industry – technology is as instrumental to your workplace as the product you manufacture or the service you offer.

Amy Zukerman

SMART QUOTES

Having addressed what smart organizations need to do to invest wisely in technology, manage their development professionally and deliver it so that it meets the needs of those who will use it, there is still one aspect that must be dealt with – how to manage it once you have it. To ensure that it is well managed the smart organization needs to consider:

• How it should organize to manage technology.

- How to get the most out of its technical resources; the people who are needed to manage the technology.

- How to ensure it future proofs its investments and maintains an eye on the changes in technology that will impact it in the future.

This chapter deals with the first two points and Chapter 9 addresses the strategic management of technology.

Organizing for technology management

Smart things to say about technology management

If you don't understand the business and how technology supports it, then you won't be able to manage your technology for competitive advantage

When it comes to how technology should be managed, organizations have three basic options:

- *Centralize* – the responsibility for the IT infrastructure and information systems development and maintenance activities rests with the IT department.

- *Decentralize* – the end-user departments develop and maintain their own information systems without input from a centralized IT department.

- *Outsource* – the development and maintenance of the IT infrastructure and information systems is transferred to a third-party supplier.

Before looking at the third option in a little more detail it is worth tracing the history of the debates and approaches corporations have used to organize their technology functions, which until recently focused on the first two options.

The end-user of the 1950s was, as with the IT professional, an expert in computing. It was not only sufficient to understand the domain in which they were working, but they also had to understand the technology. With the development of new techniques, tools, programming and operating systems, together with the increasing power and improvements in the price–performance ratio, there was a greater use of computers within organizations by non-experts. As a result, end-users were no longer required to understand the technology, as the packages they used removed them away from the operating system by way of the interface. The proliferation of computers and the perception that they could be used for almost any purpose led to increasing demands from the user community for more and more systems. The mushrooming of requirements overloaded the IT department, who were increasingly spending a larger proportion of their time maintaining existing systems. This, in turn, led to the end-user becoming more and more dissatisfied with the lack of service and poor response. Subsequently, there was an increasing backlog of systems development work that, when completed, often failed to meet the original user requirements, was delivered late, and was often substantially over budget. Furthermore, claims from the user community that the IT department were incapable of developing systems to meet their business needs resulted in them taking the development into their own hands. These problems, coupled with the more favourable cost of computing power, led to the phenomenon of end-user computing. This term refers to the development or coding of information systems by the user or non-IT professional. End-user computing, which began in the mid-1980s, has increased substantially, so that it is now a significant proportion of an organization's technology budget.

The perceived benefits of this shift to end-user computing were many-fold:

- By developing their systems themselves, users were able to reduce the development backlog, thereby releasing the centralized IT department to take up some of the other outstanding projects.

- Users believed that better systems were ultimately produced because they, as users, were able to understand the requirements of the system far better than anyone else – there was no gap in the business knowledge, so often encountered with the centralized IT department's approach.

- Users believed they could develop systems faster, although this was often achieved through the avoidance of standards and procedures.

- They believed that training improved, because they were training their fellow users with the same background and experience.

However, users often cited these benefits without fully comprehending the wider issues which were just as important in meeting their needs, but, more critically, the needs of the organization. The proliferation of computers, software and systems within end-user communities soon became a major problem. Without an overall strategy within which new equipment could be procured, and new systems developed, duplication of hardware, software and data resulted. Such duplication had serious implications for the organization, and not just in terms of cost. For example, it was possible to bombard the same customer with identical marketing and sales literature because similar data would be held in multiple – and often localized – databases. More importantly, this data was often out of date and inaccurate. Furthermore, the approach to development that avoided the IT depart-

SMART QUOTES

The IT department will be the focus for the majority of public and private sector outsourcing projects over the next three years.

Andy McCue

ment's standards and procedures often resulted in poorly engineered systems that were also difficult to maintain. This defeated the objective of bypassing the IT department in that these systems were often incapable of meeting their business objectives.

The pendulum swing from centralized to decentralized and back again is an ongoing issue for organizations because there is no one best way to manage technology. In the end a balance has to be struck between flexibility and control. As we can see, there is no easy answer and with the emergence of outsourcing this has become more complex. Because outsourcing has grown in popularity, it is worth covering this in more detail.

Smart things to say

When it comes to outsourcing, know your motives

As we have seen, organizations struggle with the management of technology, but for some it has proved to be too difficult. Consequently, many have turned to outsourcing as a way of making it someone else's problem. This is reflected in the significance of outsourcing both in terms of its market and of the companies that provide outsourcing services:

- Ninety per cent of US corporations outsource one or more of their support activities.

- The worldwide spending on outsourcing is expected to reach $150 billion by 2003 (Gay, 2000).

- The UK's outsourcing industry grew by 19 per cent in 2001 to £6.9 billion.

Although outsourcing can be beneficial, many organizations have rushed into the process without really thinking about the longer-term consequences. This is reflected in a survey of IT directors who attended a recent IT Director's Forum. It is clear from this that managing outsourced arrangements is far from easy. Most who responded felt that defining realistic and fair service-level criteria was key to having a successful relationship with the third-party outsourcer. Unfortunately, getting such service guarantees in place is not a simple affair. For example, negotiating a service-level agreement is a complex, time-consuming and costly task. The difficulty lies in creating a balanced agreement that does not favour either the outsourcer or the client. Failure to do so leads to protracted legal disputes and long-term problems, and, most importantly, a lack of trust. As a result, many firms turn to specialist lawyers who can ensure the contract and agreements are balanced and fair.

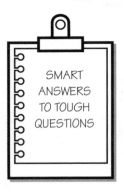

SMART
ANSWERS
TO TOUGH
QUESTIONS

Q. How can productive customer–supplier relationships be established?

A. Great customer–supplier relationships depend on mutual trust, which requires both the supplier and customer to adopt the right behaviours.

Suppliers must:
- Continuously learn from the experience.
- Listen beyond product need.
- Orchestrate their internal resources to deliver excellent service.
- Align their strategic objectives to the customer.
- Understand the financial impact of decisions.
- Adopt a consultative approach to problem solving.

Customers must:
- Involve suppliers in relevant strategic decisions.
- Seek opinions from their suppliers.
- Ensure the relationship is a shared by
    1. jointly defining the relationship goals
    2. designing and monitoring relationship metrics
    3. proactively dealing with any relationship barriers.

Another realization is that outsource contracts do not save money. Considering that many are sold on this basis and organizations seek them out because they seek cost savings, this should come as a surprise for some.

The reason why costs are rarely reduced include:

- Costs are poorly monitored and controlled.

- Additional time and effort is required to monitor, enforce and manage the contract.

- Exit strategies are rarely considered at the start of the contract.

- External staff are usually more costly – after all the third-party supplier also has to make a profit.

SMART QUOTES

Just as with the centralized and decentralized options, success with outsourcing cannot be guaranteed. There is no simple answer, and if organizations wish to outsource some or all of their technology management, they need to consider the impacts very carefully. The decision to outsource should follow a set pattern.

1. Assessment

First, it is necessary to assess how good your existing technology management arrangements are. This can be achieved by comparing your current performance against external benchmarks. This is essential to ensure there is no knee-jerk reaction to IT problems or to what is happening with your competition. There are plenty of wrong reasons to outsource, including:

- *Fear* – normally because there is a feeling of a loss of control.

- *Imitation* – following what the competition has done.

- *Frustration* – washing their hands of their troublesome technology.

- *To focus on the core business* – which is not technology. Although care should be taken to understand how technology supports your core business processes, as this should not always be outsourced.

- *To save costs* – as we saw above, rarely the case.

Benchmarking involves assessing how well you manage your technology by comparing your own organization's performance against others in the same industry sector or of similar market size. Assessing such things as staff numbers, IT spend, percentage of spend on infrastructure and

SMART
PEOPLE
TO HAVE
ON YOUR
SIDE

Sylvia Codling
- Managing director of The Benchmarking Centre Ltd.
- Author of *Benchmarking*.
- Founder of The Global Benchmarking Network.
- Believes benchmarking is one of the most effective ways of transferring knowledge and new ideas across and between organizations.

innovation can be instructive. Also, understanding what other organizations do provides an indication of how much change is required to bring your performance to an acceptable level. The danger of outsourcing for the wrong reasons is that you pass your problems onto a third party who will probably charge you for unravelling the mess they have inherited.

2. Decision

Next, if you still wish to outsource, you need to decide which aspects of your technology you wish to include. There are a myriad of options. You can outsource every aspect of your technology from its development to its maintenance, from the infrastructure to its strategic direction. Anything is possible. The key to deciding on what's best depends on how important technology is to your business (see Chapter 1) and on how well you faired during the benchmarking exercise. At this stage it is important to understand what the objectives for outsourcing are going to be.

3. Selection

Having made your decision you need to select your supplier, of which there are many. The choice depends on a number of factors, including:

- Expertise

- Service delivery

- Cost savings

- Supplier's reputation

- Existing relationships

The location of outsource suppliers is increasingly less of an issue and indeed may result in substantial savings. For example, there has been a growing trend to employ Indian outsourcers who are not only highly effective, but also significantly cheaper than their US or UK counterparts. But caution has to be exercised (see Smart People to Have on Your Side: *Computer Weekly*). The process of selecting a supplier usually involves issuing a request for information which seeks to reduce the number of suppliers to a manageable number before issuing an invitation to tender/request for proposal, which will require the suppliers to provide highly detailed information about their services and how they will meet the requirements laid out in the tender document. As the popularity of outsourcing has grown, the opportunity to source software development overseas has increased dramatically.

SMART
PEOPLE
TO HAVE
ON YOUR
SIDE

Computer Weekly

Computer Weekly has come up with the following advice for managing overseas outsourcing:

- Check the background of each supplier.
- Be prepared to send programmers back if you are not happy.
- Make sure the specifications are tightly worded and clear.
- Make sure your own processes are slick and in order before you outsource them. Outsourcing is not a panacea.
- Cultural and communications barriers take time and effort to overcome.
- Make sure the offshore team understands the business requirements.

4. Negotiation

Finally, there is the contract negotiation which, as we saw earlier, can be a minefield, especially if it is perceived to be unfair on either the supplier or customer. Contracts can be very complex and it is important to have the appropriate legal expertise on hand. Standard contracts can literally fill an entire shelf, and organizations may find it too time consuming to read these, preferring to trust the supplier and sign the contract after only a cursory read. This is often fatal. More time spent up front reviewing the contract can save immense trouble later. Once the contract has been struck, care should be taken to ensure that it is well managed and that costs do not escalate. This should include performance regimes and exit strategies.

William Ury
- Co-founder of the program on negotiation at Harvard Business School.
- One of the world's leading negotiation experts.
- Author of *Getting to Yes* and *The Third Side*.
- Believes that successful negotiations depend on:
  1. Separating the people from the problem.
  2. Focusing on interests and not positions.
  3. Ensuring there is more than one option.

SMART PEOPLE TO HAVE ON YOUR SIDE

Outsourcing should never be considered an easy option because it rarely offers long-term cost savings. Indeed, it requires management overhead at a cost of around 10 per cent of the annual contract. It is also important to remember that an inefficient or poorly structured IT function is rarely improved through outsourcing. In general, if it is broken, it is far better to fix it before handing it over to a third party.

Like the centralized and decentralized models of technology management each of these has an upside and a downside. Careful consideration of these should be made prior to deciding on which combination would be best for the business. For completeness these are summarized in Table 7.1.

Table 7.1 Technology management options

Approach	Pros	Cons
Centralized	• Economies of scale • Simpler to implement organization's strategic direction • Reduces duplication of effort • Reduces costs • Balances resource needs • Allows consistent approaches to be applied to the development process	• Harder to implement local requirements • Slower development times • Increased systems development backlog • Powerful functions' needs met before those with less influence • Increased the disconnect between business and technology • Reduces flexibility
Decentralized	• Allows lower-level empowerment and decision making • Improved focus on local IT needs • Better fit between business and technology needs • Better working relationship between business and IT • Improved system design	• Limited or no development standards • Proliferation of systems to support individual needs • IT spend invisible • Local systems not aligned with the rest of the organization • Harder to cope with complex inter-system relationships • Leads to islands of information, and data integrity problems • Increases overall (organization) IT spend
Outsourced	• Reduces IT infrastructure costs • Increases speed of information systems development • Improves service quality and productivity • Allows access to leading edge technology • Reduces technological risk • Increases technological flexibility • Eases the overall management activity associated with IT	• Increased costs (over the long term) • Increased risk • Loss of internal technical knowledge • Loss of flexibility (especially if locked into a long term contract) • Access to technical talent within the vendor is often limited • Increased information management complexity through having to manage a third party vendor relationship over which there is limited control

Ironically, despite the massive shift to outsourcing and more recently application service providers (ASPs – see below), centralization is on the increase as organizations have recognized the need to control one of their most important resources. Ultimately, of course, the way in which an organization manages its technology relies on such things as:

- The level of dependency it has on technology.

- The nature of its market and how technology supports or shapes it.

- How well it manages its technology now and how well it needs to be managed in the future.

And it should be remembered that it is possible to mix all three models if it is capable of adding value and supporting the business. Therefore it is possible to outsource the non-core elements of your technology, such as communications and infrastructure (servers, networks, telephony, office automation and so on) while still retaining control over the applications on which your business depends. Critical to making any decision is understanding what technology is core to the business. If the infrastructure as well as the applications are business critical, which they are in some regulated industries such as pharmaceuticals, then neither should be outsourced. Conversely, if technology is only ever going to play a minor role within the business, then it can be outsourced. It is generally a good idea to undertake an assessment of your technology to determine how best to manage it. This can be done by executing the first step of the outsourcing process.

New and emerging models for technology management

More recently, there has been a refinement to the outsource model, itself a response to the advances brought about by the shift to the New

Economy, the Internet and improvements in communication technology. Within the ASP model, the software is operated on the service provider's hardware while the application is delivered to the client's desktop (be this a PC, network computer or any other configuration) using a secure private network or public Internet connection. The ASP model provides a number of benefits:[1]

1. It removes the need to purchase software and maintain it.

2. It eliminates the internal costs associated with the administration of desktop software

3. It provides smaller organizations with access to the types of application that are more accessible (because of the investment required) to the larger enterprise, such as enterprise resource planning (ERP) applications.

4. It allows access to systems and applications that are infrequently used. This is possible through a pay per use billing system which allows companies to use software applications that they would have never purchased or developed because of the infrequent usage.

5. It allows access to skilled technicians and software experts without recruiting, training and retaining them yourself.

The ASP model is still relatively new and a small number of organizations have adopted this approach to running their business applications. According to technology analysts such as the International Data Corporation and the Yankee Group, the market for ASPs is predicted to grow significantly over the coming years, but like every prediction one needs to take it with a pinch of salt. Should the organization wish to adopt the ASP approach to technology management they would need to follow a similar process as they would for traditional outsourcing. And as with

[1]For a detailed discussion on application service providers, see Toigo (2002).

> ### Computer Weekly
>
> *Computer Weekly* has come up with the following list of issues to consider when choosing an ASP:
>
> - Does it have the right staff? It is essential that the provider has the breadth and depth of technical skills required to provide an excellent service.
>
> - Will it survive. The ASP model is new and as a result a number of service providers went out of business, expecting far too many customers than they actually attracted.
>
> - Is the contract clear? Like an outsource it should be clear, supported with service-level agreements and termination and liability clauses.
>
> - Will it share risk? Ultimately the best ASPs are those that are willing to share some of the risks of the business.
>
> - Are the system requirements clear? As we have seen in Chapter 4, if poorly articulated these can cause big problems.
>
> - Is it secure? If you are allowing the service provider to host your systems, security in its widest sense is vital.
>
> (D. Bradbury, *Computer Weekly*, 15 Mar. 2001, p. 42)

outsourcing it is important to think long-term, not just short-term. This helps to ensure that you outsource for the right reasons.

Looking to the future and how technology might be managed five to ten years from now suggests that things might change once more. The latest concept that is gaining credibility is utility computing, where organizations will be able to pay for what they use. So rather than having everything in-house or outsourced, organizations will literally be able to turn on their computing and technology needs in the same way we turn on a tap for our water. Such a concept is very new and may not take hold until 2007 or beyond, but many of the large technology service

You pay for electricity, water and telephone services according to how much you use, so why should the same not be true of IT? Until now, the concept of IT as a utility has been more talked about that practised. But this is changing as hardware and software have become more sophisticated, standardized, and robust. Increasingly, IT companies are starting to offer a range of services for which they charge a per-use basis.

Andrew Fisher

providers such as Unisys and IBM are already working out what this means for the way their services are delivered and paid for.

Utility computing is part of a long line of approaches that are designed to achieve value for money out of technology while addressing the dual tension of flexibility and control. At the heart of utility computing lies Grid Computing, whose name comes from the UK's National Grid, which provides electricity to homes and businesses across the country. Just as electricity is drawn from the network of power stations that are dotted around the UK, so too will computing power, although in this instance it will be drawn from the millions of PCs and servers. As with the concept of utility computing, the development of grid computing is some years away, but once it does appear it will have profound effects, not least on the role of the technology expert who will have to become significantly more business aware than they are now. It's adapt or die.

The SETI project

The SETI project harnesses computing power over the Internet by hooking into PCs overnight in order to process vast amounts of space data to look for extraterrestrial life forms.

Managing the technologists

Establishing an effective organizational model for managing technology is clearly important, but of greater importance is establishing the ground rules for managing the technologists. Organizations continually struggle with how to manage their technology staff, often preferring to leave them to their own devices. As we saw earlier, in the 1950s organizations were not really sure how to handle the new technology that had started to impact their operations. And because they did not fully understand how it worked, they decided to leave it, and those who understood it, alone to make their own way in the organization. In doing so however, they allowed it to develop its own unique culture disconnected from the rest of the organization and focused on technology rather than business imperatives, and ways of working that, even now, appear to be quite alien from the rest of the organization. In essence, they have created their own unique culture.

> Computer scientists deal with artefacts created by man and not existing independently in nature. Because of this arbitrariness, computer professionals have considerable latitude in formulating new terms and assigning new names. This provides a seemingly interminable stream of idiosyncratic nomenclature which descends all too easily into jargon.
>
> Brooke

SMART QUOTES

Although an organization may appear to have an outwardly homogenous culture, it is in fact far more heterogeneous in nature. Any organization consists of various departments and functions established to provide a particular internal, or external, service. And, although all geared toward the stated ambitions, goals and objectives of the organization, each has

Watts Humphrey

- Fellow at the Software Engineering Institute, Carnegie Mellon University.
- Author of numerous books on software engineering and managing technical people.
- Believes that without motivated and capable employees, no technical organization can prosper.

its own set of values which, along with its activities, help to define its own unique culture – the way we do things around here. For example, the Finance Department has a fundamentally different culture to the Marketing Department because it focuses on the financial health of the organization, while Marketing focuses on the development and marketing of the organization's products, as well as establishing and promoting its brand. Although such differences in culture can create friction from time to time, they rarely lead to major organizational problems. Unfortunately with technology and IT in particularly, the opposite is true. There are number of reasons for this:

- Unlike other organizational functions, IT is omnipresent in that most, if not all, other parts of the business depend on the IT function for their own operational efficiency. Such dependency on a single function is not replicated anywhere else in the organization. This brings IT's particular strain of culture into constant and sharp relief – it cannot be ignored. Other functions may clash from time to time, but because of the infrequent nature of these clashes, they are able to coexist in relative harmony. Outsourcing IT will not solve the problem. All that happens here is that you are dealing with a third party's IT culture not your own.

- Whereas the general concepts and processes of, say, marketing and finance can be understood by the layman, those of IT are less accessible. This is partly due to the speed at which IT changes versus the relative stability of other organizational departments, but it is also due to the language they use, which tends to have a much higher percentage of jargon when compared to other functions.

KILLER QUESTIONS

Do you manage the technologists, or do they manage you?

- IT is essentially about change, whereas other units are usually about operational efficiency and stability. The introduction of any new technology invokes change that creates turbulence within these generally stable environments. When this fails to deliver, something needs to be blamed – IT is the obvious candidate

- The typical IT professional is more likely to associate with their profession than the company they work for – ask anyone what they do, and whereas the average employee will respond with "I work for company x", the typical response from the IT professional is "I work in IT", or "I'm a database administrator" and so on.

- Those that seek a career in IT do so because they find the allure of

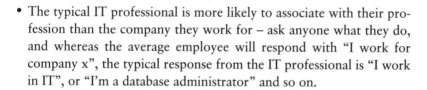

Q. Which technologist would you like to work for you –

1. One that is able to articulate a need in business terms?

2. One that is able to articulate a need in technical terms?

A. Clearly, technical knowledge is important, but if it cannot be translated into everyday business language, it will be lost on the average employee. Moreover, it will lead to too strong a focus on technology (and not product) and result in a technologically focused solution that is difficult to use and will fail to add real and lasting value.

SMART ANSWERS TO TOUGH QUESTIONS

So how do you motivate these strange self-possessed, iconoclastic people? The short answer is, you don't. Not directly anyway. What you do instead is what they do in the best technology companies: provide the kind of environment where people are free to motivate themselves. Create a work environment where they're inspired to produce their best because it's challenging and fun, but also because they can see it's to their advantage to do so.

Carol Kinsey Gorman

technology irresistible. They feel more comfortable communicating with their machine than their colleagues. This is a significant problem and one that has major implications for the organization, not least in the problem of IT and business being unable to communicate on the same wavelength. The bigger problem lies in the constant desire to work on new technology which leads to an increasingly larger number of legacy systems developed on legacy platforms and with legacy languages. As more applications are developed, the available resource pool diminishes as more staff become involved with maintaining the active systems rather than developing the new.

IBM

- Global technology and professional services firm.
- Established a programme to spot and develop their outstanding technical talent.
- Found that highly talented technical professionals were best identified by their peers and managers.

Recognizing that technologists are different is a key step in being able to manage them. But in order to get the best out of them it is useful to understand what their characteristics are and how best to hone their talent. It is also important to develop hybrid skills that allow the technologists to understand both the technology they develop and the business they work within. This latter aspect should also include managerial and leadership development.

The whole concept of hybridism is in hot debate, especially in the UK. The idea that the problems can be resolved through hybrid skills is perhaps a little naïve. It should be clear by now that technology management requires a multitude of disciplines if it is to be successful. Moreover, not every IT person has the ability, or desire, to become a hybrid. Therefore it is better to provide career paths that meet the needs of the hybrid and the more business-focused technologists as well as the purists, who would prefer to remain active and deeply involved in the guts of the technologies they work on. That said, It is important to spot your technologically talented employees because, as the organization becomes more dependent on technology, you will need smart and talented people to ensure it is capable of supporting the business. We cannot dismiss the technologists as they are too important. What we

Many technical professionals don't have a real understanding of the marketplace, the competitive situation, and the economic climate. They will perform better with this knowledge – and have a fuller understanding of the value of their contributions.

Taylor-Cummings

have to do is to become smart at spotting, managing and developing them.

Here are some of the qualities of a top technologist:[2]

- Independent minded

- Creative – willing to explore and experiment

- Driven by complexity

- Motivated and self confident

- Capable of identifying and analysing a problem and developing a solution to it

Smart things to say

To become a great technologist requires that you have a combination of talent, experience and motivation

Developing technologists probably requires more effort than the average employee. The reasons, as we saw previously, revolve around their personality and desire to be deeply involved with the complexities of technology and how it can be applied to complex problems. It is important, therefore, to provide suitable career paths that will broaden their experience and capabilities. Unlike the business person, the latent capabilities of the technologist need to be coaxed out. The smart organization thus needs to design career paths that incorporate development opportunities that will broaden the technologist's capabilities and which are still able to offer them the challenges they seek.

In this way the smart organization can move away from the mindset that allows Peters' Principle to persist in which a person rises to their level of incompetence – usually based on their technical, not business capabilities.

[2]For a detailed discussion on identifying talented technologists, see Humphrey (1997).

Instead, a developmental period is required in which the IT expert is able to augment their skills and become a rounded business professional.

The next chapter deals with the specific role of the CIO as this is pivotal; but, as we shall see, the CIO has a very different focus than the pure technologist.

SMART QUOTES

Technocrats are deadly when they're in charge.

Henry Mintzberg

8

Reinventing the CIO

The emergence of the CIO

As technology, and particularly information technology, has become vital to the organization, so has the realization that it requires strategic management and executive-level visibility. Organizations started to appoint CIOs to drive the strategic management of technology through-out the organization during the 1980s. Their brief was simple: manage the IT operations and provide advice on IT's use across the business. The principal reason for bringing a senior IT professional onto the board was therefore to give IT an appropriate voice in the governance and direction of the organization, especially in relation to how it could be used strategically. However, in the main this has not worked because of the gulf that has developed between the CIO, who has been and still is in most instances a technologist, and the rest of the board, who were still sceptical of the ability of technology to add value. Some of the reasons for this disconnection include the CIO's technical focus, their narrow experience and their use of technical jargon. However, I believe there are other factors, including:

- The recognition that IT is now a significant factor in organizations and this has disrupted the existing balance of power between the functions, and the rest of the board don't like it.

- The board feel uncomfortable with IT because they don't or won't understand it – it exposes a weakness which they do not wish to confront.

- The board still sees IT as a support function, rather than one that provides direction. As a result, they tend to treat the CIO accordingly by focusing him on the operational problems with IT rather than its strategic value and direction.

- Although the CIO may believe that IT is adding value to the organization, the rest of the business does not. For example, one survey found that although 85 per cent of IT managers believed they had a role in convincing senior management of the importance and benefits of new technology, only 48 per cent of board-level directors viewed the technolgists as either advisors or strategists.

- IT people feel uncomfortable sitting on the board because they lack the general business acumen required to govern the organization. As a result, their contribution becomes narrowly focused on technology which reinforces the disconnect and the board's preference for the CIO to discuss operational rather than strategic issues. The CIO would be wise to understand what leadership entails – before they join the board (see Smart People to Have on Your Side: Robert Terry)

This lack of connection is serious. For example in one survey, 47 per cent of CIOs believed their main problem was the culture gap between IT and business professionals, and 56 per cent believed it was damaging the organization's ability to gain competitive advantage (Price Waterhouse, 1993). What they fail to see, of course, is that they are contributing to it, and that the disconnect at board level influences what happens lower down in the organization and how the rest of the organization relates to IT.

The state of the nation

CIO Magazine conducted a survey into the state of the CIO during 2001. This sought to explore the trends of the role and what was critical to its success. The key findings were as follows:[1]

- *Communication.* The survey found that the majority of a CIO's time was spent communicating with three key stakeholder groups: the board, their staff and suppliers. The clarity of communication, particularly in expressing ideas and direction were seen to be essential as was the ability to negotiate, but not just with suppliers – there is plenty of internal horse-trading required.

- *The ability to think and strategically.* With IT increasingly taking on a strategic role within organizations, the need to understand the competitive landscape and the business's strategy is considered a critical component to managing IT strategically. This means that the CIO needs real business understanding and depth, not just the traditional technical focus. This breadth of understanding is considered to be important in order to develop and maintain productive working relationships with the rest of the board. Unfortunately the survey found that most CIOs did not have strong business knowledge or experience.

- *Staff management.* With many organizations facing skills shortages, the ability of a CIO to retain her best technical staff and bring on her

[1]For the full survey results, see *CIO Magazine*, Issue 1, Mar. 2002.

most able resources is vital. And, despite the softening of the IT job market, this was still considered to be important.

- From a career perspective, very few CIOs see themselves as the future CEO. The majority were happy to remain in the CIO role even if they changed jobs.

- The CIO's role and general job description does not vary much between organizations.

- Technical skills are less important than being able to communicate and understand strategy.

It is clear the CIO is increasingly fulfilling an essential role within most companies and it is also clear that the role of the CIO needs to evolve from one that is predominantly technically focused to one which is more business oriented. This is a significant challenge, not just to those who are, or aspire to be a CIO but also for the organization and how it spots and develops its future board-level talent. Smart technology management has to begin with the board, and having an appropriately qualified CIO is an essential determinant of success. This is, of course, not lost on the CIOs themselves, as one recent survey by the London Business School and personal development network Impact discovered. The survey found that CIOs recognize they need to improve their leadership and management skills but don't know where to go to get the appropriate training. The survey also highlighted the desire of most CIOs to be more strategic and less technological. With this in mind it is worth exploring where the CIO role is heading.

All change for the CIO?

As IT has taken on an increasingly significant role there has a general

> Organizations cannot afford to have CIO standing for "career is over". Far better for it to mean "career in overdrive". Only than can you attract the talent you need.

shift in thinking about the CIO. No longer just destined to be the technologist on the board, there is a belief in some quarters that they are the new CEO. This was particularly the case during the height of the dotcom boom, when e-business was purportedly redefining the business landscape and raising the profile of the CIO. This battle-cry soon died down with the demise of the dotcoms and in any case was fundamentally missing the point about the CIO's characteristics and capabilities. As we have already seen, the CIO lacks the qualifications and experience required to be an effective CEO. Indeed many existing CIOs do not see themselves as the next CEO, preferring to remain in the world in which they are comfortable. Plus we have to remember where most CIOs have come from. Starting work as a system programmer or database administrator and moving through systems analysis, team leading, project management and IT management before becoming the CIO is too narrow a career path to make them a well-rounded CEO.

Despite this, there is an increasing need for CIOs to unshackle themselves from the narrow technological view they hold and move increasingly into one that encapsulates both business and strategic management. Again *CIO Magazine* suggests that, for some at least, this is already happening. CIOs are having to widen their capabilities to focus much more on the strategic management of IT rather than the narrowly defined operational role they have taken to date. To that end an increasing number of organizations are recognizing that the task of the CIO cannot be fulfilled within a single person and are introducing another role, the chief technology officer (CTO). The CTO's responsibilities lie in the operational domain, freeing up the CIO to take on the strategically important role at board level. How successful this will be can only be judged over time, but in order for the CIO in particular to be successful, he must report to the CEO. Unfortunately many still report to the chief financial officer (CFO). This automatically creates problems because of the different focus the CFO has when compared to the CEO. CFOs by their very nature are concerned about the financial governance of the business, which usually means establishing strong controls over spending, and when it comes to downturns in business cycles, cost cutting. This creates problems for the CIO who needs to be investing in new and probably complex technologies in order to drive the future growth of the business. The combination of the cost focus of the CFO and the generally poor track record of technology investments leads to a significant problems for most CFO–CIO relationships. To break out of this, the CIO needs to create a culture of high performance. They must also report directly to the CEO, or if this is not possible, the chief operating officer (COO) if one exists.

Charles Wang

- Chairman and CEO of Computer Associates.
- Author of *Technovision*.
- Believes that the fundamental problem that organizations have with IT is due to the business and IT communities failing to communicate.

SMART PEOPLE TO HAVE ON YOUR SIDE

Robina Chatcham of the UK's Cranfield School of Management believes that the CIO of the future needs to display the following attributes:

- They must clearly understand how their business works, which includes the competitive (and hence external) environment.

- They must be able to use IT to make the business more successful.

- They must be a leader with vision, passion and empathy.

- They must embrace politics, but also collaborate.

- They must sharpen up their image, in essence playing the part of a senior executive.

- They must have credibility with technical and non-technical people.

- They must be capable of translating technical matters into business language.

- They must be willing and able to issue challenges to the business and contribute to business ideas.

Thus the CIO of the future needs to be less concerned with the day-to-day operation of the IT infrastructure and more focused on working with her fellow board members on navigating the organization through its uncertain future. This can only be achieved if the CIO has credibility and wide experience. The Hays survey mentioned in Chapter 1 also highlighted a growing recognition that the influence of IT over the organization will continue to grow. A full 63 per cent of respondents believe this is because IT will become more central to the business and almost half felt that the CIO will become a core business strategist. This makes reinventing the CIO a pressing issue for most businesses.

SMART QUOTES

In letting general managers get away with not committing to projects, CIOs are putting their projects and careers at risk and ensuring that IT is kept in the back office – with all the other administrative functions.

Susan Cramm

The other thing the CIO needs to do is to start to behave like any other director, which according to the UK's Institute of Directors should include the following qualities:

- Strategic awareness
- Objectivity
- Communication
- Individual responsibility
- Customer focus
- Self-discipline
- Teamwork
- Creativity
- Perspective
- Breadth

CIO Magazine
- A magazine dedicated to the role of the CIO.
- Has a wealth of information, career advice and information which every CIO needs.
- Can be found at www.cio.com.

SMART
PEOPLE
TO HAVE
ON YOUR
SIDE

Smart advice for the smart CIO

Taking the state of the nation and the advice of Robina Chatcham into consideration, here is some smart advice for the CIO:

- Refuse to become the whipping boy for every technology ill that befalls the organization. Your job is to steer the organization through the turbulent technological times ahead.

- Demystify technology for the rest of the board, and make them aware that technology can be of benefit to the organization, but can also create problems.

- Make the board aware of the impacts of IT dependency, and make them aware of their role in ensuring the application of technology is successful.

- Be brutally honest about the costs and benefits of major technology projects. Try to avoid massaging the numbers in order to gain approval. If a

SMART VOICES

The *Guardian* newspaper

The UK's *Guardian* newspaper has underlined its commitment to IT by appointing its IT head to the board. In his previous role, he was responsible for realigning IT to the business and improving the perception of IT among the *Guardian's* staff. IT is now deeply involved with the decision-making process of where to target technology investments. Furthermore the focus on people and business skills over technology skills has ensured that new recruits are suitably adjusted to the new environment. This, at times, means turning down technically qualified candidates who are unable to speak in business terms.

(J. Wastnage, *Computing*, 8 Mar. 2001, p. 8)

project cannot be properly justified, then it may not prove to be beneficial to the firm in the long run.

- Take the time to really understand other parts of the business. Taking a genuine interest in the other key disciplines within the organization can only improve your credibility with your fellow board members. As the impacts of technology within the economy continue to rise, the criticality of your role will increase.

- Don't believe that CIO translates to "career is over". Instead, use your combined business, technology and strategic understanding to guide the organization.

- Don't be lured into the leading edge. Just because you are perceived to be a technical expert, don't fall into the trap of hyping the benefits of the latest technology. One of the key skills you bring to the board is your ability to assess technology and provide a balanced argument as to its acceptance or rejection within the organization.

- Ensure that IT in its entirety is aligned to the organization's objectives and that it is sufficiently flexible to change as the organization changes.

Because the handling of information is core to business, CEOs should become engaged in IT as in any other important business function. Too many CEOs, though, have remained distant from IT. Information systems are often thought of as too complex and unmanageable. Making IT relevant to business strategy seemed like an intractable problem. Discussions always seemed to get bogged down in acronyms. However the CIO tried to say it, the real message was that old systems were too complex, too expensive, and too inflexible to meet new of changing needs.

Bill Gates

- Ensure the organizations' information is current, relevant and accessible. Information in all its constituent forms is essential for the smooth running of the firm. One of your jobs is to ensure the underlying technology is supportive of information needs, and sufficiently flexible to change as the information needs change.

- In these turbulent times, the ability to apply technology successfully is critical to the organization. Use your skill, knowledge and judgement to ensure the organization uses IT wisely and profitably.

- Persuade the CEO to recruit a CTO as this will free you up to take on the strategic role you were recruited for.

Advice for the Smart CEO

If we assume that the CIO reports directly into the CEO, then here is some smart advice for the CEO to get the best out of the relationship:

- Don't abdicate responsibility for IT to the CIO and the technologists. With the success of the organization increasingly dependent on technology, it is irresponsible to ignore the consequences, by burying your head in the sand and believing that it has nothing to do with you. With 73 per cent of directors believing IT is of little strategic value (Gorman, 2000), it might be prudent to be one of those that believes it is strategically important. IT is here to stay, and it should be seen as a long-term enabler, rather than a short-term fix to business problems.

- Before you invest in any major technology project, or one that involves a significant IT component, challenge the business case. If you are uncomfortable with it, ask that it be revisited. You should only bet your company on those projects that are realistic in their objectives and their outcomes.

- If you don't have time to investigate the viability of a technology project, employ someone who can.

- At the time of the business case, consider the implications on the organization of late delivery, and failure. In doing so you will automatically consider the risks.

KILLER QUESTIONS

Can you honestly say that the CIO is a respected member of the board?

- Before you embark on any major technology project, ask yourself this one question: is the environment in which this project is going to be executed conducive to success? If it is not, then it is your job to ensure it is. If it is, ensure it stays that way.

- Take an active interest in the costs of your major technology projects, and especially the benefits. Don't take benefit claims at face value: demand concrete reasoning to justify them, and ask that the impacts of any slippage and change in the projects are reflected in the benefits case. This will help to make any decisions about termination easier and avoid the temptation of believing in jam tomorrow.

- Be prepared to pull the plug on a project that is spiralling out of control. It doesn't matter if it is an internally or externally run project, the outcome will still be the same – failure. It is far better to terminate it early, when you still have some money left to finance other projects.

- Embrace technology and take the trouble to gain a basic understanding of some of its upsides and downsides. The technologists and salesmen only ever talk in upsides. Recognizing there are downsides adds balance and allows you to challenge the technologists rather than accepting what they have to say at face value. This should force the technologists to be more realistic in their claims.

- Don't believe that any problem can be solved by technology alone, most will not.

- Take with a healthy pinch of salt any claims that suggest a new technology will radically improve your organization's prospects. Many are unfounded, unjustifiable and lead to disappointment.

- Introduce real accountability for the success of technology projects, and make this effective across the whole organization – including the board. This means being prepared to implement sanctions where project personnel have deliberately lied about the status of their project, and where third-party suppliers have kept progress hidden from view. Unprofessional behaviour should be penalized, not accepted.

- Accept that some projects will inevitably fail, and when they do, learn from them. Do not react by blaming, sanitizing or forgetting. But, when there is a need for accountability, enforce it.

- Expect the best of your project managers, and don't compromise. Project management is a crucial element to any technology investment so make sure your project managers are suitably trained to meet the challenge. And, if you use third parties, make sure they are too.

- Don't always believe the advice of the experts, and if you consider their advice to be suspect, then you are probably right – you may have learnt your lesson from the dotcom boom and bust. If you haven't, perhaps you ought to.

Generating a culture of smart technology management

The CIO's role should be to create a culture of smart technology management within the organization. It is their responsibility to ensure that technology is aligned to both the strategic and operational goals of the enterprise and that new technology is implemented and applied in a professional manner. This means taking the advice outlined above and developing a culture of competence and service excellence.

We can learn a lot from the high-tech companies that typified the dotcom boom. Although many failed, they were able to generate an effective culture that was focused and fun. This type of culture is mirrored in the majority of high-tech companies and is something that the CIO and CEO should be interested in. According to Carol Kinsey Gorman (2000), there are eight culture commandments that all high-tech companies take seriously:

- Egalitarianism

- Freedom

- Informality

- Trust

- Responsibility

- Teamwork

- High performance

- Fun

Taken together, these eight dimensions of culture can be very powerful and many of the household names within the high-tech industry – including Peoplesoft, Lotus, Texas Instruments and Cisco – live by them. If they can develop a high-performing technology company, why can't non-technology companies? I believe they can, but they must have the right leadership. Which is where the CIO comes in. If a similar culture were developed inside the technology function it is highly likely that the technologists would be well received by the rest of the business and the disconnect between them would reduce. Developing a powerful and effective culture also means ensuring there is a link between the

SMART
PEOPLE
TO HAVE
ON YOUR
SIDE

McKinsey and Company Inc.

- Strategic management consultancy.
- Believes there are four IT cultures:

  1. IT Stars – organizations that tend to be effective at IT without unnecessary spending. These organizations are very business focused and service oriented.

  2. Big IT Spenders – organizations that are also effective at IT but in this case spend more to achieve the same results as the IT Stars. They tend to invest in most new technologies and generally prefer to invest in expensive bespoke software rather than off-the-shelf packages.

  3. Cautious IT Spenders – organizations that control their IT costs very carefully and do not tend to spend more than they have to. The real issue for the Cautious IT Spenders is that they fail to invest in technology that can be used to drive the business.

  4. IT Laggards – organizations that have significant IT spend but derive little or no benefit from it. Such wastage is due to poor internal processes and project management. Such organizations do not track their IT investments and fail to exploit technology as much as they could. For them IT becomes a money sink.

technology culture that the CIO develops and the rest of the organization. Once again this means that the technology function and the products it delivers and maintains must be aligned to the strategic and operational objectives of the business.

In conclusion, a lot rides on the role of the CIO. The CIO is an important board member and one who cannot be ignored or sidelined. CIOs need to be given their head and the freedom to add the value necessary to shape the business and to ensure that the organization's internal processes and systems are as efficient and effective as possible. This requires that the CIO has a real voice at the board and is taken seriously. The smart organization knows this and uses the CIO to good effect. The next chapter looks at an equally important topic in smart technology management – keeping track of the future, which as we have seen is a core role of the CIO.

9

Keeping Track of the Future

The genie is out of the bottle. There is no doubt that technology in all its forms will continue to affect us all in subtle and not so subtle ways. The key thing is to learn how to deal with it. But, success in technology is not just about following all of the advice covered so far, as there is one element that is still missing – futurology. Because technology has the ability to transform organizations and severely disrupt the status quo, the smart organization needs to keep track of the technologies that are likely to affect it directly, or those which it could exploit. For example, as far back as the 1990s, the Japanese had drawn up a list of technologies that were expected to drive future wealth and prosperity. Not surprisingly these technologies are familiar to us all and include biotechnology, telecommunications, robotics and computers. The skill of managing their impacts involves

> ## SMART QUOTES
>
> You can't solve a problem with the same thinking that created it.
>
> Albert Einstein

Today's microprocessors are almost 100,000 times faster than their ancestors of the 1950s, and when inflation is considered, they cost 1,000 times less. So what can we expect of the next fifty years?

understanding how they will change over the coming thirty to fifty years.

To do so requires us to:

• Think in terms of scenarios.

• Develop strategies that add real value.

• Maintain the strategy once it has been set.

• Minimize the risks that technology imposes on the organization.

The responsibility for keeping track of the future lies with the CIO, the board and the technologists. It is not something that can be done in

SMART VOICES

Nanotechnology in the oil industry

Nanotechnology, working at sizes of 10^{-9} m, is helping to transform the oil industry. A US alternative energy company recently signed a deal with China's largest coal company to build a plant to liquefy coal and transform it into diesel and gasoline. When nanoparticles are used with fossil fuels they can harness the power of virtually all the atoms used in the catalytic process, thereby reducing costs and improving efficiency. But nanotechnology will not stop there. It is already starting to transform the energy generation business, computer memory and solar power. If it lives up to the hype, nanotechnology may have the ability to transform most, if not all, industries that are based on the creation of products.

isolation by any one individual. After all, there would be little point in analysing technology without modelling its effects on the business strategy or wider business environment.

Before discussing these aspects in a little more detail it is worth highlighting some of the pitfalls of the strategy development process, as once known they can be avoided. There are two camps, both of which purport to be the most effective at developing strategies. The first is strategy as planning. This tends to be heavily focused on information, tends to be a top-down driven exercise, and is also systematic and structured. The second is strategy as process. Here the emphasis is on managing the environment and as a result tends to be more systemic and emergent with little importance placed on planning. Irrespective of preference, strategy formulation depends on the combination of both and a strategy without one is usually suboptimal. And, regardless of your choice, it is important to avoid the two common pitfalls with strategy. The first is that it can be seen as, and indeed become, an ivory tower. This normally occurs when strategy formulation is an academic exercise and has little or no contact with, or relevance to, the real world of the organization. New MBA graduates often fall into this trap, spending vast amounts of time and energy crafting a wonderfully intellectual strategy full of wishful thinking that will never be implemented. Ultimately strategy needs grounding in the reality of the organization, not something from a textbook. This pitfall is exacerbated when the strategists are too remote from the organization and do not take the trouble to understand the way the organization functions.

Equally disastrous, and to some extent a factor of ivory-tower thinking, is strategy without planning. Here the strategy is produced and literally thrown over the wall to the business for it to implement. This usually results in departments doing what they like and implementing change on a piecemeal basis. Unsurprisingly such projects are often duplicated by other departments leading to overlaps, gaps, inconsistencies and wasted effort. In the end, strategy needs to be operationalized through projects and programmes of change.

SMART VOICES

ASIMO

ASIMO, short for Advanced Step In Innovative Mobility, is a 1.2-metre proto-type robot developed by Honda Motor Co.'s Wako Research Centre just outside of Tokyo. The robot is able to greet guests and shake hands. But this is just the beginning. The scientists at Wako are busy developing humanoid machines that will be capable of undertaking household chores. The science fiction of robots is moving into reality through increasingly powerful chip technology and reducing costs. Some believe that Japan's personal robot market could become an $8 billion per year market and that robots will become as accepted as the personal computer. Of course there are still plenty of hurdles to over-come, not least creating artificial intelligence. The impact of these robots on business as well as home lives should not be overlooked.

(C. Lee, Time, 26 Aug. 2002)

Visions of the future – scenarios and scenario planning

We all struggle with the sheer amount of information that we have to deal with, even on a daily basis. As we saw earlier, information continues to grow exponentially and we cannot hope to absorb and understand the implications of everything around us. However, we have to become better at assessing the changes that are likely to occur and that will ultimately affect us all. Scenario analysis is an increasingly popular tool for attempting to understand the future and what it might mean for

KILLER QUESTIONS

How will you avoid future shock?

the organization. And rather than beginning with the past and projecting forward, scenarios start with the future and project back. Their real beauty is that they provide the basis for creative thinking, by building consensus as to the likely futures the organization will face. They are also a very useful way of testing the robustness of any strategy, be it business or technology. It must be recognized that developing scenarios takes time because it requires a significant amount of research into the factors that are affecting the future.

When creating their scenarios most companies start with similar factors and these usually include most of the following:

- Demographics, including the ageing of the population, immigration, shifting patterns of population within countries and so on.

- Environmental change, which is increasingly important for many companies and includes such things as pollution, global warming, depletion of natural resources and so on.

- Economics, which is increasingly global and connected.

Kees Van Der Heijden

- Professor of General and Strategic Management at the Graduate Business School, Strathclyde University, Glasgow.
- Previously in charge of Royal Dutch/Shell's scenario planning.
- Author of *Scenarios: The Art of Strategic Conversation.*

- Science and technological change, including trends such as biotechnology and IT.

- Government and international legislation and control.

- Customers, their behaviours and expectations.

- People in general, in terms of their attitudes and behaviours.

The analysis of these and other trends allows the organization to develop a number of scenarios or future worlds in which they will have to exist and hence adapt to. Scenarios use combinations of the identified factors and trends and serve to describe, not predict, the future using a small number of key drivers. These drivers are derived from the analysis of the trends and factors and are usually binary in nature (see the Smart Voices on the United States Air Force for an example).

Here are some of the rules that should be applied if the scenarios produced are to be valuable:

- At least two scenarios should be developed, as one would not be sufficient to model the uncertainties the organization faces.

- They must be plausible. If they are too "off the wall" no one will be able to relate to them and they will be destined to become shelfware.

- They must relate to the organization's situation. If the scenario describes something that is unrelated to the business, it will not have the desired impact on creativity and thinking.

Each scenario has a theme and a name that people can relate to (for example, Caring Corporates) and each major factor (technology, economy, government and so on) is described within the scenario's theme. The implications on the organization are also identified, although at this stage they are usually at a high level. Once a more detailed strategy has been developed, it is normally tested against each of the scenarios; this helps to test its robustness under a variety of circumstances. It also helps to prepare the organization for the uncertain times ahead. The value of scenarios is usually illustrated by Shell, who used them to predict and then manage the impacts of the oil crisis in the 1970s. Shell's development of scenarios involved its operational managers, who had to describe how they would respond to the futures provided to them during their long-term planning process. As a result, Shell was able to respond much faster than their competitors during the oil crisis. Over the years Shell has benefited from scenarios in five ways:

1. It found that its strategic decisions and project investments were more robust under different futures, thereby future-proofing them.

2. It became much better at thinking about the future.

3. They enabled Shell's manufacturing personnel to become more perceptive and recognize events as being part of a pattern, rather than isolated incidents.

4. It was able to set a wider context for decision making down the line instead of dictating precise and direct instructions.

5. It was able to use scenarios as a leadership tool.

After more than 25 years of scenario planning, Shell would not manage its strategic risks any other way.

United States Air Force

The United States Air Force (USAF) has developed a number of scenarios for 2025. The scenarios were designed to examine the concepts, capabilities and technologies the United States will require to remain the dominant air and space force in the future (up to 2025). In order to develop the scenarios, the USAF analysed trends in computer hardware and software, space, communications, media, nanotechnology, medicine, technology, international relations, the environment, education, population and the economy. Having analysed these drivers, it came up with three key drivers against which the scenarios would be positioned:

1. American World View. This driver described whether the US would have a domestic or global perspective. If domestic, the US would focus on internal problems rather than involving itself in world affairs. A global world view implies the US would seek a world leadership role

2. ΔTek. This was defined as the ability to employ technology, which would either be constrained, with technology taking on a more evolutionary growth path, or exponential, where technology changes very rapidly and is widely exploited

3. World Power Grid. This dimension was all about power in whatever form it took and could either be concentrated or dispersed.

These drivers resulted in the following scenarios:

*   Gulliver's Travails – a world of rampant nationalism, state- and non-state sponsored terrorism, and fluid coalitions.

*   Zaibatsu – a world dominated by corporate economic interests.

*   Digital Cacophony – a world where technology dominates and accelerates.

*   King Khan – a world dominated by the Asians.

*   Halfs and Half-Noughts – a world in turbulence as it transforms itself into an information-based society. Those who cannot change fast enough join the growing ranks of the have-nots.

*   Crossroads – a decision point from which the other alternate futures might be reached.

The USAF is actively using these scenarios to prepare for the future ahead.

(Col. Joseph A. Engelbrecht Jr et al., Alternate Futures for 2025, 1996)

Scenarios are increasingly popular within government and military circles and are gradually taking hold within industry. The smart organization will understand their value and use them where appropriate. And with technology serving to increase the speed and impacts of change, every organization would be wise to apply scenarios at least occasionally.

> The world is about to exit the Information Age and enter the new era of "Bioterials." The marvels of the Bioterials Age will be more global in their impact than the Internet. Its products will be more important than fire, the wheel or the car and more productive than today's biggest supercomputers. The Bioterials era will generate more new knowledge in a shorter period than history's collective wisdom and the power of its technologies will eclipse that of the combined armies of the world.
>
> Richard Oliver

The critical role of strategy and strategic planning

The prevailing view from the New Economy was that strategy was dead. Organizations were no longer expected to set out their medium- to long-term strategic objectives and follow them. Instead it was fashionable to provide direction on the fly without any consideration of its effects on the organization's stability or profitability. Such an attitude to strategy resulted in many organizations rushing headlong into new technologies, including e-commerce and mobile telephony. Although some have been successful, the majority have not and vast sums have been wasted in the process. It is premature to write off strategy because it remains an essential part of any organizational planning process. Without it, it is impossible to make decisions that make sense in the medium term or to test out investment decisions. The fact that organizations are now dependent on IT should come as no surprise to anyone. What should come as a surprise is that relatively few organizations manage their IT as a strategic resource and even fewer actively set IT strategies. This clearly has to change.

The starting point for developing technology (IT) strategies is to consider them in the wider context of business strategy. There is often a distinction made between information systems (IS) strategy and IT strategy. The former views technology on a wider basis, taking into consideration the business, its drivers and priorities, while the latter is more technology focused, looking at hardware, software, infrastructure such as communications and networking, as well as the standards and

SMART
ANSWERS
TO TOUGH
QUESTIONS

processes used to develop and implement new systems. IS strategies also tend to be more focused on the organizational components such as staffing, skills, structures and how these are impacted by technological change.

Developing an effective and relevant technology strategy usually follows a number of steps. The actual timing of these will vary from organization to organization and will depend on such things as their complexity, the nature and use of technology, their market position and so on.

1. Information gathering

This is an essential first step. Information gathering involves understanding the business context, which should come from the organization's vision and strategy (if they have one). This establishes the core competencies of the organization, their current position, where they wish to be in five to ten years from now and what their major priorities are for the years ahead. This stage of the strategy process should also focus on understanding how well the current technology serves the needs of the business. This will include developing an understanding of the current technology and systems landscape within the organization and should involve making an assessment of its strengths and weaknesses. The business strategy may well have been developed off the back of scenarios and these will provide a useful backdrop to the development of the technology strategy. This stage will involve interviewing senior executives across the business to ensure their needs and interests are captured

Pricewaterhousecoopers Technology Centre

- Part of the global accountancy and business advisory firm.
- Publishes the *Technology Forecast* on an annual basis.
- The forecast provides an insight into the direction of technology and the processes behind it.

2. Establishing the future direction of technology

This involves understanding what the future of technology might hold (that is, what is possible) as well as what is practical. The use of technology road mapping techniques, where technology experts provide a view of technology trends can be useful. There are also plenty of organizations that now offer similar services including Gartner and Giga. This information should be used to establish what future systems and technologies might be useful to the organization.

3. Perform a gap analysis

The next stage is to perform a gap analysis by comparing the business vision, the current state of the organization's technology and where the future of technology lies. This will help assess both what's possible and what's achievable. What's achievable is constrained by such things as funding, capability of staff and how reliable the technology is likely to be, especially when new. The gap analysis will also provide a measure of risk, as if the gap between the current state and strategic direction/needs of the organization is large it could impose unacceptable risks to the business. This stage is critical because it will help assess some of the risks and priorities before moving onto formulating the strategy

4. Formulating the IS strategy

This will map out the strategies that will be followed over a typically three to five year period. Such strategies should include information on:

- The drivers that underpin the strategy.

- The objectives.

- What constraints exist which limit the strategy in any way.

- The risks and uncertainties that still have to be resolved as the strategy is implemented.

- Any assumptions that have been made when formulating the strategy.

This must link to the business strategy, although it should be recognized that some aspects of the technology strategy may lead to changes in the business strategy. Keeping an open mind is therefore critical as is being prepared to iterate. At this stage the strategy is focused on the systems that are required rather than focusing on the standards and detailed technologies that will be applied. This means that the strategy has to be articulated in terms that the business understands to allow it to be widely reviewed and debated. The IS strategy will outline the major programmes and projects of change required to deliver it. So, as well as describing what the organization wishes to achieve, it details when it will be done

5. Formulating the IT strategy

A second tier strategy that is more focused on the guts of technology still has to be produced. It includes such things as:

- Standards for technology platforms

- Operating systems

- Office automation software

- Security

- Development and implementation methods and tools

- Disaster recovery and business continuity

- Data management

- Information architectures

- Skills and staff requirements

Although the IT strategy should support the IS strategy, it is primarily geared to ensuring that standards are set and maintained and the underlying infrastructure required to support the information systems and the business are effective.

At the end of the process the organization should have a business-focused IS strategy, high-level implementation plan and a more detailed technology strategy. The story does not end here because keeping track of the future also requires the organization to ensure the strategy is well implemented and that impacts on the business are monitored and played back into the strategy.

Maintaining the strategy

A strategy without any means of monitoring its implementation is useless. Many organizations suffer from this type of problem and allow the strategy to become shelfware. This gives it a bad name and leads to businesses abandoning the strategic planning process. If the strategy is to continue to be of value it must be maintained. This involves updating it on an annual basis, taking into account progress and changes in the external environment. To achieve this requires the organization to monitor its projects and programmes of change (see Chapter 5) and measure their impact on the operations of the business. As we saw in Chapter 5, many projects fail to deliver the changes expected and if this is the case, the strategy will be impacted and must be updated. Equally important is the need to maintain an external perspective to monitor any major events or changes that could impact the strategic direction of the organization and its use of technology. Naturally if the organization has developed a number of scenarios this should help to pre-sensitize the strategy, but even if these are in place the external environment still needs to be monitored. The use of balanced scorecards and IT balanced scorecards can be particularly helpful. These should include a number of key performance indicators against which trends can be monitored and actions taken when they deviate from their expected path. Such scorecards should address:

- The effectiveness of the change as it is implemented.

- The reliability of the systems as they are developed.

- The service provided by the technologists to the business.

- The investments and ongoing costs associated with technology.

- The learning and development of all who come into contact with the new technologies implemented as part of the strategy.

A basket of good measures will ensure feedback from the operations of the business is combined with feedback from the strategy. This will keep the strategy fresh and make its maintenance far simpler.

SMART QUOTES

> Most Internet start-ups failed because they were based on the mistaken premise that the Internet represented a revolutionary new business model, which it didn't.
>
> John Cassidy

Don't bet the company – managing the risks of technology

Investing in the latest technology without giving it sufficient thought, or indeed without assessing the risks that it might pose, is a fatal mistake that many organizations make. Take 3G mobile technology, take e-commerce banking, take government IT projects. All have common factors, and it would have been far better to understand what the risks were before investing so heavily in technologies that were destined to be failures or were too disruptive to the status quo. But this is too simplistic a statement; hindsight is such a wonderful thing. The most important skill when considering future technologies and their impacts is to assess how it might affect the organization. Many of the risks associated with technology have already been addressed in earlier chapters, as have some of the difficult questions that the smart organization needs to ask itself both before and during any technology investment. However, there is one other area that needs to be considered before the organization decides to invest in the latest technology – the skills available to implement it and maintain it. This is a strategic issue, and this is why I have included it within this chapter. The problem is that technology fatigue does not just affect business people, it also affects the technologists. Organizations must recognize that their technologists too have their fair share of problems with rapid technological change. Unfortunately many expect them to be able to apply the latest techniques, tools and technologies, often without any formal training. This leads to the following types of problem:

- *Ignorance of prevailing knowledge.* Technology professionals may not be aware of the full extent of the new technologies and techniques available, even though the organization expects them to understand all aspects of IT. This can place them in a difficult position when they are expected to implement a new technology which they know little about. With faster cycle times, and shortening project horizons, there is often no time to gain the necessary understanding prior to attempting its implementation; the project becomes the training ground.

- *Failure to use prevailing knowledge.* Although aware of current tools, techniques and technologies, the organizational pressure for rapid implementation often means there is no time to use them. Such time

SMART
PEOPLE
TO HAVE
ON YOUR
SIDE

Stan Davis and Christopher Meyer

- Authors of *Blur: The Speed of Change in the Connected Economy.*
- Believe that technology will continue to change and blur the world in which we work and live.
- State that speed, connectivity and intangibles combine to blur the clear lines that used to distinguish buyer from seller, product from service and employee from entrepreneur.

pressure means there is little time to train staff, which in turn reduces the chances of delivering the project successfully. Indeed, a recent report from Kennedy Research Group suggests that, as organizations clamour for more and more IT, they, along with consultancies, are fielding second-rate staff. The same report goes on to cite a civil suit that has been filed by W. L. Gore Associates against Deloitte Consulting, who, according to Gore, had assigned unknowledgeable and inexperienced consultants to install PeopleSoft human resource software to integrate payroll automation. According to the suit, the resulting chaos led to payroll accounts that did not balance, employees not getting paid, and vacation and health benefits that could not be tracked.

SMART QUOTES

Changes in our business surroundings have been equally surprising, and often frustrating. On one hand, business is now conducted at a pace and with an accuracy that nineteenth-century scientists and visionaries from Charles Babbage to Jules Verne did not dare to predict. . . . On the other hand, the benefits of automated data and word processing have not been quite as expected. The revenge effects are physical . . . the revenge is also financial.

Edward Tenner

- *Conditions beyond prevailing knowledge.* This is the classic leading-edge project that typically involves pioneering activity and trail-blazing by the IT expert, using hitherto untried and untested technologies, tools or techniques.

The role of senior executives

Setting the technological direction for the business is not a role for the CIO alone. It is clear from the previous chapter that the CIO needs to take on a strategic role, but this role should not be performed in isolation. The other board members must be involved. According to James Cox, author of *Executive's Guide to Information Technology*, senior executives need to consider three things when it comes to dealing technology.

1. Standardize. One of the problems organizations have faced is the hunt for the elusive magic bullet, the enabling technology that will allow systems to be developed faster and to a higher quality. Such searching is usually in vein and it usually leads to more and more tools and techniques being used, thereby diluting the skills of the

---

Xerox Parc (Palo Alto Research Centre)
- Sits at the heart of Silicon Valley.
- Invented the personal computer in 1972.
- Laid the foundation for the laser printer and the Macintosh computer.
- Believe that the microchip will become part of the fabric of our lives.
- Continues to research into new technologies and how they impact us all.

SMART
PEOPLE
TO HAVE
ON YOUR
SIDE

technologists. It is far better to select a small number, develop deep skills in them and then apply them professionally.

2. Senior executives they must recognize that in order to develop IT systems effectively they must ensure that a rigorous process is followed. This means following the advice laid out in Chapters 3–7.

3. Senior executives should encourage the technologists to seek out new technologies and to continue to assess their standards and processes. This ensures that the organization gets best value from their technologists and that the strategy is properly aligned.

SMART QUOTES

Despite industry calls for usability the computing world of the 1990s turns out to be a patchwork of stand-alone machines and networks, professionals and amateurs, always in a state of tension between the productivity benefits greater power brings and the learning and support costs that it requires.

Edward Tenner

This completes the smart thinking on technology management. This has not been a simple how-to book, but it has provided an expansive review of what constitutes successful technology management from assessing which investment to plumb for to how it should be managed. The majority of organizations fail in one or more of the areas discussed within this book, which means they must have something to learn. So by way of summing up, the final chapter looks at the ten steps to successful technology management.

10

Looking to a Rosy Future

We are living in an increasingly wired world in which our personal and working lives are ever more entwined with technology. Many of us are still uncomfortable with it, but unfortunately we all have to deal with it. Some say that it is a generation thing and that future generations will be more familiar and happy with the effect that technology has on their lives. I don't believe this to be true. Technology always has the ability to shock and surprise. We saw this during the agricultural and industrial revolutions and we are seeing it now. Although we may be comfortable with the technology that we grew up with, we usually have problems with that which follows. The problems are, of course, not just associated with our perceptions of technology and its disruptive ability; it has a lot to do with the way in which technology is developed, introduced and functions. These are

> SMART QUOTES
>
> Books will soon be obsolete in the schools.
>
> Thomas Edison (1913)

Larry Keeley

- Member of the Doblin Group
- Believes that high-technology businesses require three qualities to be successful:
  1. Capability – what technologists bring to the business, in essence what they can deliver.
  2. Viability – what the business contributes, in other words what is saleable.
  3. Desirability – what the designers create, which means understanding what people (the customers) want.

major factors in the way we perceive technology and influences how willing we are to use it. For the majority of us, and particularly at work, this has been an uncomfortable experience and one which leaves a bitter taste.

It would be wrong, and indeed impossible, to turn back the clock, so the best option is to become smarter at how we develop technology, how we introduce it and how we work with it. I believe the majority of the issues we face with technology are soluble so long as those charged with its development and introduction manage the process carefully. With sufficient rigour and attention we ought to be able to look forward to a rosy future in which we are happier with technology's role. Naturally the complexity of technology will not permit everything to function correctly all of the time, but it is an appropriate aim all the same. There are ten steps to success, which, if applied, will help the management of technology to be a smoother process:

1. Ensure technology is on the organization's strategic agenda

This means giving technology issues sufficient air time at board level, making the board responsible for the strategic use of technology and ensuring there is time and effort spent on understanding how the technology developments of the future may impact the organization. This may be the role of the CIO and CTO, but they should not be expected to achieve everything on their own. With technology playing an increasing role, the responsibility rests with the board as a whole. It is not sufficient to just set the strategic agenda, as this will not allow it to be appropriately implemented. Therefore, as part of the process, it is vital that the technology strategy is translated into actions, projects and measures that will allow the board to monitor progress as the strategy is realized.

2. Act like a venture capitalist

It is clear that more care needs to be taken when investing in new technology. Certainly some speculative investment is required, as this is a

---

Alvin Toffler

- One of the earliest futurologists . . . but with a healthy dose of reality.
- Author of future shock – a book about what happens to people when they are overwhelmed by change.
- Defines future shock as the shattering stress and disorientation that we induce on individuals by subjecting them to too much change in too short a time.
- Always believed that people need to come to terms with the future in order to help them cope with the personal and social changes that accompany it.

SMART
PEOPLE
TO HAVE
ON YOUR
SIDE

central theme to innovation. But what we must move away from is the slapdash way most organizations manage their investment portfolio. Too many rush headlong into their next technology investment without assessing why or understanding what value the technology will bring. Acting like a venture capitalist is an attitude that prevents rash investments (although there are dangers, as we saw in the dotcom boom) and phases the funding for the investment to allow termination should the technology or the project designed to deliver it prove to be inappropriate. This mindset also reduces the likelihood of the irrational behaviour associated with over commitment from taking hold.

SMART EXAMPLE

US state schools

Since 1990 US states have spent more than $40 billion on computers, networking and software for their schools. At least 50¢ of every dollar spent on educational supplies now goes on technology. Students are able to use the latest PCs and laptops loaded with the latest office automation and other software. The problem is that there is no conclusive proof that this technology is actually helping students to learn, and in some cases it is believed to be hindering the process. Moreover the benefits do not seem to be matching the costs. For example, the $250 million spent by the New York public school system could have paid for 7,800 more teachers, 5 million textbooks or 10 million hours of tutoring. The technology companies claim that without technology, students will be left behind and will be unable to read or write. Others disagree.

(J. Landry, *Red Herring*, Aug. 2002)

3. Maintain a sharp focus on benefits throughout the entire lifecycle

Every technology investment should be delivering benefits to the organization. Smart technology management requires the enterprise to

McKinsey

- Surveyed leading companies within the manufacturing sector.
- Presented their research results in the book *Do IT Smart*.
- Developed seven rules for superior IT performance:
  1. Make IT a priority in product development.
  2. Integrate IT into marketing, sales and service.
  3. Use IT selectively to integrate order processing across the company.
  4. Shift the focus of IT in administration to business planning and management development.
  5. Make IT a top management affair.
  6. Create a customer-oriented IT service network.
  7. Introduce integrated standard software on a fast-follower basis.

identify realistic benefits at the time of the business case. Most business cases lack defined benefits and where they are present, these tend to be artificially high. Such window-dressing may be a great idea to secure initial funding, but in the end it helps to waste money on a product that will deliver substantially less than was stated. To avoid some of the usual issues associated with costs versus benefits, flip the equation by discussing the problem and benefits first. This will help to set the budget and ensure a realistic perception of benefits is established. And remember, once the project has started the benefits need to be modelled and tracked throughout, and some kind of measurement framework needs to be in place to monitor the realization of benefits once the project has completed

4. Think product, not technology

This is a great way to move away from the technology-centric thinking that has dominated organizations over the past fifty years. A product view provides a number of distinct benefits, not least the ability to bring into sharp relief the whole issue of who will be using the technology once it has been delivered. It also reduces the likelihood of vapourware, bloatware and shelfware, all common outcomes when it comes to software products and systems. Once you start thinking in product terms you will become more successful at understanding how products are developed, delivered and exploited. In many respects thinking in product terms is central to smart technology management

5. Always manage your technology projects with care

We all know that technology projects are notorious for escalating costs and timescales. We must accept that the complexity of technology and the way organizations wish to employ it make the majority of technology projects difficult undertakings. To be successful necessitates the application of strong and first-class project management skills. Project management is not just about schedule management, nor is it about technology. It encapsulates much of the softer issues that cause technology projects to fail. Realistic planning, sound risk management, understanding and dealing with politics and communication are all part of the process.

Smart things
to say about
technology
management

Beware the Titanic effect. This states that the severity with which a system fails is directly proportional to the intensity of the designer's belief it cannot.

6. Don't forget reception strategies

An over-the-wall, or an "if we build it, they will come" mentality serves no purpose. If organizations wish to get the most value out of their technology investments they must attend to the people who will be excepted to use it. We can learn much from product innovators who take the trouble to prepare the market before a product is launched. In a similar way the smart organization can prepare the user community by understanding their needs, managing expectations and working carefully with the stakeholders to address their concerns and issues. In this way the technology (assuming it works well enough) will be more readily accepted. In the end, one of the reasons why organizations experience problems with such things as resistance to change is because they have failed to develop a suitable reception strategy. Once again, thinking in product terms can be very helpful here because it forces the project team and technologists to think about the real people rather than abstract users

7. Don't believe that technology can solve every problem; it can't

Many people still hold the belief that technology is capable of solving any problem. Clearly this is not the case, and there are plenty of examples within this book that demonstrate this. However, the fact that this type of thinking is still as prevalent as it has always been suggests that technology is more seductive than we think. Technology certainly has its place, but before you invest heavily in a new technology step back for a few moments and consider whether it is the right course of action. If you are unsure, spend some time and money checking it out a bit further.

8. Don't believe everything the technology experts say

The experts would have us believe that anything is possible now. Back in the 1980s we were led to believe that we were on the dawn of a new age with the emergence of artificial intelligence. The Japanese spent billions

Avoiding the dodos of new technology is a fine art, so be warned: the next big one is lumbering over the horizon right now. This year's candidate for early extinction is the so-called smart phone. These ridiculously sophisticated mobiles boast a plethora of features that are utterly pointless: dire digital cameras, "full" internet browsers and e-mail. They are trying to do three jobs simultaneously – those of a computer, digital camera and phone – which is like asking a doctor to put out fires and lock up villains when he is not busy icing Mrs Pethwick's veruccas. The workload is excessive and the smart phone is simply not smart enough to cope. Not only is it dumb, it is also bulky and expensive.

Barry Collins

trying to achieve it and failed. Now in the twenty-first century, the Americans are doing precisely the same. Will they succeed, where the Japanese failed? Time will tell. All technologists are hopeful and believe that the next breakthrough will be profound. The majority are wrong. However, what we do see is the gradual development of technology so that science fiction can often become science fact. The gadgets used in the early James Bond films and Star Trek seem so *passé* these days, yet at the time they were literally out of this world. The technologists can often predict the future, but they usually get the timing wrong. Equally, when we talk to software vendors they will always claim that their product is the one to beat all other products and would have you believe that it will transform your business. In some cases it ties it up in knots, which is a form of transformation, but not the one that was expected. Sure, listen to what they say, but don't believe everything and certainly do not take it at face value. Always check it out.

9. Ensure you are organized to manage technology proficiently

Smart technology management depends on how well the underlying technologies that support the business perform. This in turn depends on how well the technology support functions are organized and how technology staff are managed, motivated and developed. With options ranging from centralization to outsourcing, organizations face difficult choices. The key is to understand how technology supports and drives the business and organize accordingly. In some cases this might mean having a bit of everything, in others, just one. The key is to marry up the support function to business needs.

10. Learn to accept and embrace change

Continuous change is here to say. Alvin Toffler predicted this back in the 1970s, and our personal experiences support his view. We are in a constant state of flux and one that is unlikely to abate. What this means is that if we are to avoid future shock we must be smarter at dealing with change and learning. Organizations are continuously reorganizing, rebranding, merging, divesting and acquiring. They are also looking to technology to help them stay nimble and in business. Technology is a massive catalyst of change. The sooner we can deal with it the better.

This book has been all about helping you manage technology. The lessons we have learnt, particularly since the computer age, is that technology can be unpredictable, it is complex and difficult to harness but can add immense value. The smart organization knows that this is not a simple exercise and will apply all the smart thinking within this book.

SMART QUOTES

Here we go again...pundits can't stop hyping the business opportunities of artificial intelligence.

Geoffrey James

References

Introduction

Fran, A. (2000), "Staff hide skills from bad bosses", *The Times*, 7 January 2000, p. 11.

Johnson, L. (2002), "New technology tells bar staff how to clean up", *The Age*, 24 June, p. 3.

Kurzweil, R. (1999) *The Age of Spiritual Machines*. London: Orion Business.

Lambeth, J. (2001) "High Street chains lose high technology battle", *Daily Telegraph*, 4 June, p. 28.

Mackintosh, J. (2000) "How banking on the Internet has become a fallen icon", *Financial Times*, 27 October, p. 29.

Nakamoto, M. (2002) "On top when it comes to the crunch", *Financial Times*, 16 September, p. 13.

Newing, R. (1999) "Taking the paranoia out of knowledge acquisition", *Financial Times*, 28 April.

Wind, J.Y. and Main, J. (1998) *Driving Change: How the Best Companies Are Preparing for the 21st Century*. Kogan Page.

Chapter 1

Felsted, A. (2002) "Easyjet whips up a storm in the cockpit", *Financial Times*, 18 August, p. 10.

Forester, T. and Morrison, P. (1994) *Computer Ethics*. London: MIT Press, pp. 113–114.

Grande, C. (2001) "CityReach joins Internet failures", *Financial Times*, 29 August.

Heavens, A. (2001) "i2 plunges on software complaint", *Financial Times*, 8 February, p. 32.

Patten, S. (2002) "New M&S chief in tech gamble", *The Times*, 23 August, p. 25.

Skorecki, A. (2002) "Global settlement system for forex launches today", *Financial Times*, 9 September, p. 32.

Wiener, L.R. (1994) *Digital Woes: Why We Should Not Depend on Software*. Reading, MA: Addison-Wesley, p. 14.

Chapter 2

Gompers, P. and Lerner, J. (1999) *The Venture Capital Cycle*. Cambridge, MA: MIT Press.

Mandel, M. (2000) *The Coming Internet Depression*. New York: Basic Books, pp. 24–31.

Chapter 3

Holland, M. (2001) "WH Smith has no complaints", *Computing*, 16 December, p. 15.

Landauer, K.L. (1995) *The Trouble with Computers: Usefulness, Usability, and Productivity*. Cambridge, MA: MIT Press.

Robins, S. (2002) *The Truth About Managing People*. London: Financial Times/Prentice Hall, p. 54.

Voyle, S. (2001) "Online, instore, in profit and now in the US", *Financial Times*, 30 June/1 July, p. 15.

Chapter 4

Cooper, A. (1999) *The Inmates Are Running the Asylum: Why High-tech Products Drive us Crazy and How to Restore the Sanity*. Indianapolis, IN: Sams (Macmillan Computer), pp. 123–201.

Cooper, R. (2001) *Winning at New Products: Accelerating the Process from Idea to Launch*, 3rd edn. Cambridge, MA: Perseus, pp. 23–24.

Durham, P. (2002) "Hutchison admits 3G problems", *Sunday Times*, Business Section, 28 July, p. 1.

Chapter 5

Coleman, S. (1992) "CS90: could have cost $10 million?" *Computer Weekly*, 20 September.

Egan, G. (1994) *Working the Shadow Side: A Guide to Positive Behind-the-scenes Management*. San Francisco: Jossey-Bass, pp. 196–211.

Keil, M. (2000) "Cutting your losses: extricating your organisation when a big project goes awry", *Sloan Management Review*, Spring.

Kennedy, S. (1992) "What went wrong with CS90?" *MIS*, May.

McConnell, S. (1996) *Rapid Development: Taming Wild Software Schedules*. Microsoft Press, pp. 379–384.

Simmons, A. (1998) *Territorial Games: Understanding and Ending Turf Wars at Work*. Amacom.

Chapter 6

Brown, A. (1995), *Organisational Culture*. London: Pitman.

Cleland, D. (1988) "Project stakeholder management", in D. Cleland and W. King (eds), *Project Management Handbook*, 2nd edn. New York: Van Nostrand Reinhold, pp. 275–301.

Moss Kanter, R. (1983) *The Change Masters: Corporate Entrepreneurs at Work*. London: Routledge.

Pinto, J. (1994) *Successful Information System Implementation: The Human Side*. Upper Derby, PA: Project Management Institute, p. 184.

Chapter 7

Bradbury, D. (2001) "What does it take to be a good ASP?" *Computer Weekly*, 15 March, p. 42.

Gay, C. (2000) *Inside Outsourcing: An Insider's Guide to Managing Strategic Sourcing*. London: Nicolas Brealey, p. 4.

Humphrey, W.S. (1997) *Managing Technical People: Innovation, Teamwork and the Software Process.* Reading, MA: Addison-Wesley, pp. 91–103.

Toigo, J. (2002) The Essential Guide to Application Service Providers. Upper Saddle River, NJ: Prentice Hall.

Chapter 8

CIO Magazine, Issue 1, March 2002.

Gorman, C.K. (2000) *The Human Side of High-tech: Lessons from the Technology Frontier.* New York: John Wiley & Sons, pp. 11–12.

Price Waterhouse (1993), *Information Technology Review 1992/93*, pp. 24–26.

Wastnage, J. (2001) "The Guardian gives IT place on board", *Computing*, 8 March, p. 8.

Chapter 9

Col. Joseph A. Engelbrecht Jr *et al.* (1996) *Alternate Futures for 2025: Security Planning to Avoid Surprise.*

Global IT Consulting Report (1999) "IT consultants burning goodwill", November, p. 1.

Lee, C. (2002) "Tin Men", *Time* 26 August, pp. 48–49.

Chapter 10

See Landry, J. (2002), "Is our children learning?" *Red Herring*, August, pp. 37–41.

Index